D1609967

Community of Scapegoats

Community of Scapegoats

The segregation of sex offenders
and informers in prisons

By

PHILIP PRIESTLEY

PERGAMON PRESS

OXFORD · NEW YORK · TORONTO · SYDNEY · PARIS · FRANKFURT

UK	Pergamon Press Ltd., Headington Hill Hall, Oxford OX3 0BW, England
USA	Pergamon Press Inc., Maxwell House, Fairview Park, Elmsford, New York 10523, USA
CANADA	Pergamon of Canada, Suite 104, 150 Consumers Road, Willowdale, Ontario M2J 1P9, Canada
AUSTRALIA	Pergamon Press (Aust.) Pty. Ltd., P.O. Box 544, Potts Point, NSW 2011, Australia
FRANCE	Pergamon Press SARL, 24 rue des Ecoles, 75240 Paris, Cedex 05, France
FEDERAL REPUBLIC OF GERMANY	Pergamon Press GmbH, 6242 Kronberg/Taunus, Hammerweg 6, Federal Republic of Germany

First edition 1980

British Library Cataloguing in Publication Data

Priestley, Philip
Community of scapegoats.
1. Prisoners — Great Britain
2. Informers — Great Britain
3. Sex offenders — Great Britain
I. Title
365'.6   HV9646   80-40364

ISBN 0-08-025231-1

Printed and bound in Great Britain by William Clowes (Beccles) Limited, Beccles and London

Preface

THE work on which this book is based was carried out at Her Majesty's Prison, Shepton Mallet, between 1966 and 1968 and written up as a research report in 1974. Two points need to be made about the present text.

Firstly, it does not refer to something which no longer exists, or which is not recognisably the same. Prisoners continue to ask for protection under Rule Forty Three of the Prison Rules, and there is still a special wing set aside for them; now at Gloucester Prison rather than Shepton Mallet.

Secondly, the book has not been rewritten to take account of contributions to the prison literature since 1974. It remains what it was when it was first written; a description of a group of prisoners in a particular place at a particular time.

Acknowledgements

I AM grateful to the late Barry Wigginton, then Governor of Shepton Mallet Prison for making it a more tolerable place to be; to the men doing time there who answered my many impertinent questions without complaint; to James McGuire for some pertinent criticisms; to Kate Lyon for her advice and encouragement during the seven years it took to complete this study; to Pat Smith for typing and retyping the messy manuscripts; and to Ben Priestley for the cover photograph.

Contents

CHAPTER 1

Her Majesty's Prison, Shepton Mallet

"Alas that there is need of such a place on Christian soil."
                                                      JOHN FARBROTHER

THE building of the House of Correction at Cornhill in the
central Somerset market town of Shepton Mallet was begun in
1610, which makes it one of the oldest purpose built places
still in use as a prison in England and Wales. John Howard paid a
visit there and described it in his book *The State of the Prisons.*
"One day-room for men and women. Men's night-room too
close; only one small window. The women's night-room is too
little: the keeper has taken what seems to have been part of it
to make his malt-loft. He told me his prison was some years
ago so unhealthy that he buried three or four a week."[1]* Death
from the gaol fever, was counted an unavoidable hazard of life
inside until John Howard and Mrs Fry began their moral cru-
sades. But historically Shepton has also been the setting for more
deliberate kinds of deaths. According to Farbrother, writing in
1872: ". . . in 1658, Jane Brooks and Alice Coward, her sister,
both of this town, after having been examined several times by
Robert Hunt and John Cory, justices of the peace, were imprisoned for bewitching Richard Jones a boy of twelve years of
age. The former of these two was condemned and executed
March 26, 1658. This was one of the last executions for witchcraft in England. . . ."[2]
   This author also recorded his more contemporary impressions
of the prison: "Of this large and important building, if little be
said, or if its internal arrangements, economy and proceedings

*Superscript numbers refer to Notes at the end of each chapter.

1

be not minutely detailed, let a pardon be granted, for its very walls look forbidding and within its courts and corridors reigns a dismal silence, broken only by the clink of keys, the creaking of a lock, the grumbling of a heavy bolt, the measured footsteps of a warder, or more rarely by the penitential moan of some poor conscience-stricken sinner." Penitential moans have since then passed out of fashion in prison circles, but the physical description still rings true.

In 1909 a prisoner was admitted to Shepton Mallet who later wrote his memoirs under the pseudonym of Stuart Wood. "It is", he said "a grim, ugly building of grey stone. The discipline was harsh, repressive and destructive, and every day brought its hour of desperation. The Governor seemed a decent sort of fellow . . . and I was really sorry to hear later that he had put himself on the wrong side of a cell door for embezzlement."[3]

Twice in recent years Shepton's long history as a place of confinement has appeared to be in danger of ending. During the 1920's and 1930's the English prison population declined to a point where establishments were actually being closed down and prison staffs feared for their jobs. In 1935 the Prison Commissioners abandoned the prison and the Army took over the building. For the next thirty years it was an important part of the military justice system. During the 1939–45 war it served as a combined services prison for the allied forces.

It retained its physical aura: ". . . the forbidding aspect, the thick grey walls and barred gates of this ancient local prison immediately conjured up for the visitor the vision of Dante 'Per me si va tra la perduta gente lasciate ogni speranza voi ch'entrate . . .' " said an army psychiatrist who worked there.[4]

Fifty-two men are reputed to have been executed in the prison during the war. Along the back wall inside, when the coke heaps run low, marks can be seen said to have been made by the bullets of the firing squads. The shooting had to stop, so the story continues, after protests from local people. They were allegedly disturbed, not so much by the deaths of the deserters, murderers or rapists, as they thought, as by the noise of the fatal fusillades which occurred at dawn and woke them at too early an hour.

After that, the work is supposed to have been despatched on the silently efficient gallows which were housed in the angle between the small wing and the main block.[5]

The Ministry of Defence eventually ceased operations at Shepton Mallet in 1965 and the future of the prison was once again uncertain. Alternative uses for the buildings were canvassed, but at what seemed like the last moment the Prison Department of the Home Office re-acquired the site from the Army with the intention of housing within it a population as exotic as any from its past.

It had been decided that a special prison should be opened to cope with a growing problem; the segregation of men who had applied to the authorities for personal protection under the provisions of Rule Forty Three: "Where it appears desirable for the maintenance of good order or discipline or in his own interests that a prisoner should not associate with other prisoners either generally or for particular purposes, the Governor may arrange for the prisoner's removal from association accordingly."[6]

Thus number Forty Three of the Prison Rules. But behind the bland administrative prose there lies a complex and intriguing social process; a process which involves sexual deviation, violence between prisoners, group scapegoating, solitary confinement and the establishment of what amounts to a voluntary prison within a prison. In a tiny minority of cases, prison governors place men on the Rule, not for their own protection, but in order to stop their attacks on fellow prisoners. These men are known as 'governor's Forty Threes'. For the rest, the rule refers to the protection of individual prisoners from the violent attentions of their peers. It refers to men convicted of sexual or violent offences against children; to 'grasses', 'stool-pigeons' or informers; and to prisoners who have failed to honour tobacco debts or similar obligations within the inmate group. The only thing that these three groups have in common is that other inmates shun, and harry and physically attack them, sometimes with extraordinary violence.

For many years the rule was invoked for only a few prisoners, and those who applied for protection under it spent the remainder of their sentences in solitary confinement; twenty-three hours a day working and eating in single cells, and an hour's exercise taken alone.[7] For some men this degree of isolation might last for only a matter of months; for some it could stretch into years.

Whilst it remained a small-scale problem, no special provision had seemed necessary, but during the 1960's the numbers of men seeking protection began to rise. In 1965 the Prison Department concentrated a number of Rule Forty Three men in one wing at Strangeways Prison, Manchester.[8] The plan was to allow men on protection to mix with others in the same situation, freed by their common plight from the fear of attack. As between the men on protection, the Manchester experiment was reportedly a success. Normal routines were followed; meals, work, association and exercise all took place as they would in an ordinary prison. The presence of an outcast group within a large local prison like Manchester, however, continued to create problems for the staff who still had to protect them as a group from other inmates. Protection cases had to use facilities in the main prison, such as the bathhouse. They might have to go to the hospital. Visits had to be taken. On all these occasions, whether the Rule Forty Three men were moved about *en masse* or as individuals, there were risks of physical attack or if that were not possible, then a chorus of jeers and catcalls accompanied their progress around the prison. Shepton Mallet, a small and secluded prison, offered a better solution; a separate establishment set aside for Rule Forty Three prisoners.

Beginning in August 1966 the protection population was transferred piecemeal from Strangeways in Manchester to 'A' Wing at Shepton Mallet. At the same time some non-Forty Three men from the South West prison region were brought in to do restoration work on the dilapidated buildings. These men became the 'C' Wing population, forty to fifty strong, which undertook service tasks within the prison and outside work on the gardens and in the staff quarters.

As a prison population with few if any exact parallels anywhere else in the world, the Forty Threes at Shepton Mallet presented a singular opportunity to look at some aspects of the social organisation of prisons and the functions of scapegoating in human groups.[9]

Prisons by their very nature excite the sociological imagination. Not only do they contain populations of criminals who are of interest both as individuals and as the product of processes of law and order in the community, but they also constitute small-scale societies in their own right, isolated from the outside world by walls and bars and other security measures. And one of their attractions to the student of society is the ease with which they can be observed and recorded. Much of the work in this field is American and has concerned itself with four main issues: the formal organisation and power structure of the prison administration; the impact of imprisonment on the individual prisoner; the existence and nature of the inmate subculture or 'society of captives', and the ways in which these potentially explosive elements are held together in relatively stable relationships with each other. They are potentially explosive because prisons compress into small spaces large numbers of difficult and dangerous people. And they are confined in conditions which not only restrict their liberty but also impose on them a version of the monastic vows of poverty, chastity and obedience. The job of holding down this unruly population belongs to the uniformed staff of the prison: prison officers in this country; guards in the United States.

In his classic study of New Jersey Maximum Security Prison, Gresham Sykes described the guards there as pursuing a number of specific and not necessarily compatible goals.[10] Their first priority was that of security: keeping their charges under lock and key for the lawful period of their sentences. The maintenance of order within the institution came next, together with enforcement of the artificially low standard of living dictated by the administrative rules of the place. Following that, men were required to perform minimum amounts of work-like activity every day. And finally lip service was paid to the idea of undertaking some kind of rehabilitative work with the inmates.

According to Sykes the experience of regimes like these can

be summarised in terms of what he calls 'the pains of imprisonment'. These include loss of liberty and autonomy in all but the
most trivial areas of existence; fear of physical assault; and the
central problem of surviving long periods of imprisonment as
mentally intact as possible. The official advice to prisoners in
these circumstances is to 'do your own time'; to serve out
sentences in a sort of self-imposed solitary confinement. This
advice is backed up by a system of rewards for good behaviour,
and punishments of varying severity for those who break any of
the many minute rules that govern the daily life of the prison.
And in theory, prison administrators possess a monopoly of
power which enables them to impose their vision of things upon
their captives.

In practice things are not so simple. Practically every published account of prison life suggests that prisoners organise
themselves to oppose this version of reality.[11] They organise
themselves into what have come to be called 'inmate' or 'prisoner
subcultures'. These are *sub rosa* societies which exist in the
interstices of the official regime and which serve to meet some
of the otherwise unmet human and economic needs of their
prisoner members.

In American prisons, at least, these inmate societies are highly
articulated affairs. They incorporate a set of values which are
derived in part from the criminal culture outside the walls, and
which stress the importance of loyalty to inmate interests above
those of the guards, and the need for integrity in dealings between
prisoners. In practical terms these values define the staff as 'the
enemy' with whom collaboration of any kind is forbidden,
except where it might serve some illicit inmate interest. And of
all the forms that collaboration can take, the most strongly pro-
hibited is that of 'ratting' or informing on other prisoners.

Another part of the inmate code concerns the characteristics
of the 'good con'. He is a man who is 'tough' and 'sharp' and
'cool', someone who displays in his attitudes and conduct a
model of poise and self-control which can help men do their
time and come to terms with the emasculating absence of
women from their lives. Other roles, some of them less admirable,

are also described in American prison slang or argot. There are 'politicians' and 'merchants' who manipulate the administrative and economic environment to their own and other inmates' advantage. There are sexual role labels: 'wolves' and 'queens', for example; and some which indicate the violent tendencies of those to whom they are applied, e.g. 'ball-busters' and 'gorillas'. 'Fish' are new entrants to the prison community, and 'square johns' are men, typically first offenders, who retain whilst inside an attachment to the 'straight' values of the outside world. And finally there are 'rats' or informers; 'rapos' or sexual offenders; and the 'dings', a residual category of petty and inconsequential offenders who are held in contempt by everyone else in the prison. These last three groups are the American equivalents of the men who formed the basis of the Rule Forty Three population at Shepton Mallet.

Studies of English and European prison communities have failed to disclose such clearly defined social structures as those which appear to exist in the United States.[12] But the existence of Rule Forty Three cases in numbers sufficient to justify the experiments at Manchester and Shepton Mallet is a violent affirmation of the presence in English prisons of deeply held common values capable of being outraged by certain classes of offenders, and of modes of collective action through which these sentiments can be expressed.

An examination of the individual protection cases at Shepton Mallet promised to throw some light on these processes. Why, for example, had these men been singled out for violent attention from other prisoners, and by what routes had they arrived in solitary confinement at their own request? Who, amongst the general prison population had taken most interest in attacking or threatening the sex cases and the informers? In what circumstances were threats uttered and violence inflicted, and what functions do these activities seem to serve for the prison community as a whole? Why is the phenomenon apparently increasing? What is the effect of personal rejection by their fellow prisoners on men who have already been comprehensively condemned by the legal machinery of the wider society?

These questions and many others relate to the position of the scapegoats within the inmate subculture of ordinary prisons. But there is another and equally stimulating set of questions which can be asked about the possibilities of co-operation between the protection cases themselves. Do they, when freed from the immediate threat of violence and brought together in what passes for the near normal in prison conditions, begin to form a subculture of their own? If so, what distinctive features does this social system possess? What kinds of roles are available to its members? To what sorts of values do they subscribe? Are there groupings within the population? On what basis are they formed? How are relations with staff handled? And perhaps most intriguing of all, does a status hierarchy develop amongst men who have already been relegated to the bottom rungs of two successive social systems: that of society as a whole, and then that of the ordinary prison subculture?

This study raises and attempts to answer some of these questions within a descriptive account of a prison and the people in it. The data on which it is based were collected in the course of working at Shepton Mallet as a prison welfare officer between 1966 amd 1968. Since much of this work involved discursive conversation with prisoners, it was not difficult to ask about the process of recruitment to Rule Forty Three, or to discuss adjustment to the situation at Shepton Mallet. Over a period of eighteen months, sixty-five accounts were gathered in this way. No notes were taken during these interviews and they were normally written up later the same day. To them were added details from other conversations and events observed during the daily life of the prison.

Research conducted in this way is subject, of course, to a number of possible sources of bias. The first of them has to do with the recording of the material. With practice it is possible to recall and write down both the sequence and the substance of even quite long interviews. Where the bias creeps in is in the shaping and censoring of the content; a subtle and forgetful kind of personal editing. Even the language of the interviewees can be subject to retrospective correction and condensation of style. Similar difficulties occur, of course, in any treatment of non-standardised data. More 'objective' information was gathered from the official prison records of one hundred Rule Forty Three men who were at Shepton Mallet during this period. In theory totally accurate, prison files are in practice imperfect documents in which even the most basic details may on occasion be missing or wrongly recorded.

A second difficulty arose from the location of the researcher in the welfare office, which made it easier to talk to and record the views of prisoners who had personal problems which they wished to discuss; or of men who were about to be released. A third, and related problem, more diffuse and less tangible than the others, but potentially more damaging to the pursuit of objectivity in the research, stemmed from the relationship between the welfare officer and the other staff of the prison; the officers, administrators and specialists. Like all social relationships, these were at once personal, based on the characteristics of the individuals concerned, *and* structurally determined by historical features and institutional forces quite outside their control. Disentangling the two is never easy, and for those involved as interested parties in concrete situations practically impossible. No attempt will be made in this study to examine directly the role of the researcher as welfare officer, although some of the structural problems of the latter role have been discussed elsewhere.[13] On a personal plane, however, these problems are not experienced as impersonal forces with neat sociological labels, but in subjective ways best described as 'opposition', 'obstruction', 'bloody mindedness', and even 'hatred' which is the word that most readily springs to mind in connection with identifiable prison researchers like Pauline and Terence Morris.[14]

Good reasons for this apparently endemic hostility between prison staff and outsiders, especially inquisitive ones, are not immediately obvious, but they may have something to do with the unresolved ambiguities and uncertainties of the prison officer's situation. Until recently the officer's cosmology was a thing of two dimensions and coloured black and white. He occupied one of the few spaces left in industralised societies where a simplistically moral view of life was not only possible but enforced with extreme vigour. They, the convicts, were the 'baddies' and we, the officers, were the 'goodies'. Explicit rules, only lately removed from standing orders, forbade any communication between officers and men other than commands and the appropriately servile responses to them. In the past a few outsiders have attempted to import some ideas which might have served to soften the stark contrasts of the prison world. The chaplain, the medical officer, the prison visitor, the tutor organiser, all brought with them expertise based on training which was external to the prison. All, in turn, were put in their places; denied effective shares in the distribution of power and squeezed into conformist roles on the staff side of the institutional equation.[15]

Welfare officers are simply the latest in a long line of outsiders and the process of absorbing them is still continuing. Until their role is fixed as firmly in the prison firmament as that of the padre, with his prayers and private visits; or the tutor with his innocuous evening classes, then there will be conflict. But historically it is possible to discern a process by which outsiders are invited into prisons to cope with matters other than containment and are then systematically prevented from doing the work for which they were appointed. Those parts of the study which refer to prison staff should therefore be read with this background of role conflict in mind, although it is not overtly critical of them, doing, as they saw it, their duty; no more and no less.

In order to understand who the Rule Forty Three men are and how they function as a prison community it is necessary to begin with some account of the routes by which they had arrived there. Most of them start in reception.

Notes

1. John Howard, *The State of the Prisons. Warrington, 1777.*
2. John E. Farbrother, *Shepton Mallet — Notes on its history, ancient, descriptive and natural,* L.C.P., 1872.
3. Stuart Wood, *Shades of the Prison House, A Personal Memoir,* Williams & Norgate Ltd., London, 1932.
4. Robert H. Ahrenfeldt, *Psychiatry in the British Army in the Second World War,* Routledge & Kegan Paul, London, 1958.
5. The harsh reputation of Shepton Mallet as an allied military 'glasshouse' is preserved in a fictional account, *The Dirty Dozen,* by E. M. Nathanson, Arthur Barker Ltd., London 1966, and also in the film of the same name.
6. Rule Forty Three was originally in the prison rule book as number Thirty Six and its origins are shrouded in obscurity. A story which the Forty Threes themselves told was that a prisoner had once reported to staff that he was being threatened and asked to be protected. No official action was taken and he was badly beaten up. Subsequently, so it is said, he sued the Prison Commissioners in the civil courts and was awarded substantial damages. Protection status was supposedly evolved after this event. Nobody who repeats the tale is ever able to specify the prison, the prisoner or the court case in question.
7. Men who had served sentences for sex offences during the 1930's and 40's claimed that no one then cared about what they were in prison for, and that physical attacks on them for that reason alone were almost unthinkable. Some of the older men blamed the increasing violence on the growing liberalisation of the regime. Abolition of the silence rule and the introduction of association, had, according to them, allowed the prison gang and the prison bully the freedom to flourish as never before.
8. Strangeways is the large and busy local prison for the Manchester area which houses around twelve hundred men.
9. Inquiries about the protection of sex offenders and informers were sent to several prison systems in the United States and Canada and produced a variety of responses. All of them made some provision for the segregation of certain prisoners but mostly for administrative convenience rather than personal protection. Troublemakers, aggressive homosexuals and the like were segregated as were also, in some cases, passive homosexuals who might attract too much attention from others. One state prison, for example, reported a highly efficient brush factory manned exclusively by homosexuals. Of the men who themselves sought segregation, the most prevalent types seemed to be gambling debtors and the victims of aggressive sexual attention. Although the low status of pedophile sex offenders was generally acknowledged, none of the Departments thought there was a need for special and separate facilities to cope with them. The numbers involved in segregation were apparently too low. The Texas State system reported only six segregation places for a prison population of thirteen thousand.

12   Community of Scapegoats

10. Gresham M. Sykes, *The Society of Captives, A Study of a Maximum Security Prison*, Princeton University Press, 1958.
11. For example:
    Hans Riemer, *Socialisation in the Prison Community*, Proceedings of the American Prison Association, 1937.
    Norman S. Hayner and Ellis Ash, The Prisoner Community as a Social Group, *American Sociological Review* 4, 1939.
    Donald Clemmer, *The Prison Community*, Christopher Publishing House, Boston, 1940.
    Norman A. Polansky, The Prison as an Autocracy, *Journal of Criminal Law and Criminology* 33, May—June 1942.
    S. Kirson Weinberg, Aspects of the Prison's Social Structure, *American Journal of Sociology* 47, 1942.
    F. E. Haynes, The Sociological Study of the Prison Community, *Journal of Criminal Law and Criminology* 39, Nov—Dec 1948.
    Clarence Schrag, Leadership Among Prison Inmates, *American Sociological Review* 19, 1954.
    L. W. McCorkle and R. Korn, *Resocialisation within walls*, The Annals May 1954.
    Gresham M. Sykes, Men, Merchants and Toughs, A study of Reactions to Imprisonment, *Social Problems* 4, 1956—7.
    D. R. Cressey and W. Krassowski, Inmate organization and anomie in American prisons and Soviet labour-camps, *Social Problems* 5, 1957—8.
    J. Galtung, The Social Functions of a Prison, *Social Problems* 6, 1958—9.
    O. Grusky, Organizational Goals and the Behaviour of Informal Leaders, *American Journal of Sociology* 65, 1959.
    Howard W. Polsky, *Cottage Six*, Russel Sage Foundation, 1962.
    P. G. Garabedian, *Western Penitentiary*, Unpublished PhD Dissertation, University of Washington, 1959.
    Rose Giallombardo, *Society of Women*, Wiley, New York, 1966.
    Robert Martinson, Solidarity under close confinement, *Psychiatry* 30, 1967.
    H. F. Cline and S. Wheeler, The determinants of normative patterns in correctional institutions, *Scandinavian Studies in Criminology*, Vol. 2. Nils Christie. ed. Oslo University Press. 1968.
    Gordon Rose, Status and Grouping in a Borstal, *British Journal of Delinquency* 9, 1959.
    Charles R. Tittle, Inmate Organization — Sex Differentiation and the Influence of Criminal Subcultures, *American Sociological Review* 34, 1969.
    J. M. Wilson and J. D. Snodgrass, The Prison Code in a Therapeutic Community, *Journal of Criminal Law, Criminology and Police Science* 60, 1969. Besides these and many other sociological references there is a voluminous literature of anecdote and autobiography which testifies to the existence and persistence of inmate organisation.
12. Terence and Pauline Morris, *Pentonville; a Sociological Study of an English Prison*, Routledge & Kegan Paul, London, 1963; and

Thomas Mathiesen, *The Defences of the Weak. A Sociological Study of a Norwegian Correctional Institution*, Tavistock, London, 1965.

13. Philip Priestley, The Prison Welfare Officer — A Case of Role Strain, *British Journal of Sociology* 23, 1972.
14. Terence and Pauline Morris; *op. cit.*
15. Mathiesen has described some of the mechanisms by which prisons rob intruders of their professional potencies. See T. Mathiesen, The Sociology of Prisons. Problems for Further Research, *British Journal of Sociology* 17, 1966.

CHAPTER 2

Sentence by Ordeal

"Rule Forty Three's a bit like the albatross. It follows you about wherever you go like an evil curse; and whatever you do you can't shake it off."

A Rule Forty Three prisoner

Reception

Reception in prison is both a place and a process. It is where clothes are exchanged and identities transformed as men cross the line that divides the outside world from the inside. For the first-time prisoner it is frequently a mortifying experience; an unfamiliar language of degradation. For the recidivist it can represent a home-coming; a welcome back to a warm niche in a restricted but predictable social situation.

The passage of a large number of men through the prisons of reception, the local prisons which service the higher and lower courts, poses a considerable problem of logistics for their administrators. Remand or conviction, each entrant has to be logged and bathed, his civilian clothes listed and stacked in brown card boxes, prison clothes and toilet kits issued, and some orientation to the regime and the rights of inmates given. At a practical level the unending flow of new recruits is something which a system geared to an absence of positive activity finds difficult enough. But entry into prison is not just a practical management issue; it is also a status passage of crucial importance to the participants on both sides.[1] It is in fact an important part of the proceedings that they should provide a fitting climax to a whole series of ceremonies which began with the ritual phrases of arrest and continued through the formalised wrangle of the court. It is the final chapter in a series of assaults on the self-image of the subject.[2]

At some prisons the non-functional overtones of reception are enhanced by the curious arrangement of the bathing facilities. Stripped of his personal belongings and clothing, the new arrival, together with his naked companions, is faced by a row of doors. Opening one he finds a kind of slipper bath, often filled by all accounts with water that has seen better days. In this he is encouraged sometimes vigorously, to bathe. He arises from his immersion and departs, not through the door by which he entered, but through another which faces him at the far end of the bath. There, in a further antechamber, he dries himself and joins a queue for the issue of prison clothing.

Quite apart from its status implications, the purely adminis-trative burdens of reception into prison have led to a literal sharing of power which has been described in a number of studies, and to the introduction of prisoners holding key jobs in the reception area.[3] Tenure of these posts is sought after and most often secured by men with long institutional careers and a highly utilitarian approach to the deprivations and opportunities of imprisonment. Some of them lay claim to their jobs on a semi-permanent basis, vacating them during brief spells of free-dom, and returning when reconvicted to where they left off on release. The attractions of a job in reception are many: access to goods and services, for example, clean new clothes to wear, issues of supplementary clothing on release, and a thriving exchange and mart conducted with desirable items filched from the property of other and unsuspecting inmates. More than that though, there is access to information: and not simply as a con-sequence of working closely with staff, but in the form of a positive opportunity to take stock of each intake as it floods through. Interest in the characteristics and antecedents of new men is no idle curiosity on the part of the reception 'trusties'; it is crucial to their function as gatekeepers to the society of prisoners.[4]

Reception is vital to the formal system in laying down ground rules for future relations between staff and prisoners, and for allotting suitable statuses to the two sides. It is used in a similar way by the inmate culture to sort out and select people to fill positions in its own role system.

The Prison Social Order

The structure of English prison society, the one to which the reception 'cons' stand guardian, is based on a discontinuous hierarchy of offenders. At the top stand the robbers, armed or otherwise, who can point to a record of successful and lucrative offences. Below them are the frauds and false pretenders, followed by burglars and thieves, and below them again the 'slags', a broadly defined lower class of petty, failed and disordered offenders.[5] Then there is a gulf beyond which are to be found two distinct groups of prison culture deviants.

The first consists of men who have transgressed that part of the informal code which governs and protects the practical but covert activities of serving prisoners; the tobacco-currency-based economic system; the 'fiddles'; the betting arrangements; the flow of information and consumer goods through the officially impermeable wall. This might be called the 'instrumental code', and it is principally concerned with regulating communication between the informal and the formal sectors of the prison system. It proscribes close contacts with officials or other members of authority so as to minimise situations which might lead to 'grassing' or informing. Where such contacts are thought necessary for the furtherance of inmate interests, then their conduct is closely prescribed. The code is sustained by its roots in a criminal subculture outside the walls, and the oral tradition of the underworld lays stress on the unpleasant fate of those who choose to ignore its dictates.[6]

The other group comprises men who have offended against what might be termed the 'expressive' part of the informal code; that part which spells out the desirable qualities of the 'good con', who is tough, is shrewd, can 'do his bird', whose word is his bond. The members of the second group, in descending status order, have committed offences like 'ordinary' rape; violence against the elderly or the young; or sexual offences against children, down to the rape of very small girls. To the merely dishonest, who form the bulk of the ordinary prison population, neither group is seen as possessing *any* claim to ties of affinity, either of motive or of common hardship with themselves.

One consequence of this split social structure is to deny to those on the wrong side of the divide the psychic comforts which many other prisoners derive from what Sykes and Matza have described as the technique of 'neutralisation'.[7] They distinguish five types of rationalisation with which offenders customarily 'neutralise' the apparent damage done to victims and their interests during the commission of offences. They include denial of responsibility, e.g. 'It was an accident'; denial of injury, 'Nobody got hurt', 'They were insured', etc.; denial of victim, e.g. 'Those bastards had it coming to them, anyway'; condemnation of the condemners, e.g. 'Cops and judges are just as crooked as me'; and appeal to higher loyalties, 'I was only helping a buddy'. With a little ingenuity the technique can be applied to virtually any behaviour; 'They shouldn't have stood in the way', 'They were rich; they can afford it', 'I thought she wanted me to do it.' These and other rationalisations are widely used by individual offenders anxious to preserve an acceptable view of themselves and a consistent version of their lives to date. They are shared and reinforced by other robbers, thieves and frauds who face the same problem, and who seek to solve it in a similar way. The sex offender who tries to neutralise his own offences by these means must do so by himself. His definitions are shared and reinforced by virtually nobody else. They are denied and execrated by almost everyone. And as the object of this process, the sex offender must come to terms with a very low level of self-esteem.

Identification

The first problem which faces the 'trusties' in reception is that of identifying the individuals to be singled out for scapegoating.[8] Old faces have familiar labels. New ones can be placed in a number of ways. The local newspaper often provides a handy source of reference to people on trial or recently convicted. In a well-organised reception the evening paper will precede the arrival of the day's remands and convicts from the local courts. Fellow offenders committed from the same jurisdiction carry the news with them and spread it as soon as may be. Adverse attention to the convicted sex offender can even begin in the van between court and prison. The man himself, particularly a naive first offender who is disoriented by the experience he is undergoing, or who is unaware of the existence of an inmate code of values, may inadvertently reveal the nature of his offence. The simplest and surest way of all is for the reception 'cons' to read the official record of each man as he enters the establishment. Although officially forbidden, this practice figures in a number of the accounts given by Rule Forty Three men about the events which led to their applications for protection. "As soon as I went in, the screw was sat at a big table reading my record. Then he put it down and the reception 'red-band trusty' picked it up and started looking through it. I waited for a bit. I thought the screw would stop him but he didn't." Or from a written account: "I noted that, although our documents were handed by the police escort to the Prison Officer in charge, they were, after a perfunctory examination and verbal verification of sentence, transferred to one of two convicts, sitting at an adjoining table, who proceeded to place them in folders. Details of my previous convictions, my height, weight, etc., were then taken by the officer but annotated by the convicts whose function it seemed to be to attend to all documentation."

When an identity thus established is joined with other favourable circumstances, then the reaction of the reception 'red-bands' and their friends can be swift and cruel. "Six of them tried to drown me in the bath." "Then they came and broke my jaw." "You remember Marlowe, he got the boiling water over his head. He was in a hell of a mess."

As a result of experiences like these Rule Forty Three men come to fear the reception process. A non-Forty Three 'trusty' who worked in reception at Shepton Mallet described some of their reactions on arrival from other prisons: "When they come into reception they get very frightened. The officer tries to calm them down with a few words but when they have to come inside the room to strip and that door is shut, they watch it close, and you can see the fear in their eyes. Then they look at me. Sometimes after receptions I can't sleep; thinking about what they've done and the way they look in reception."

The Officer's Role

Given the extreme pressure placed on the administration by the arrival of large intakes from the courts, it seems probable that reception and other officers will be absent from their official posts from time to time. Rule Forty Three men hint that some of these absences may be strategic: "They both (reception red-bands) looked at me and said 'Oh he's one of those is he?' When I went up to the window in reception to get my things they told me to go up and see the medical officer and come back to collect my things. They gave the things to everybody else before they went up so I thought there must be something wrong. There was an officer standing there and he heard what they said so he must have known what was going on. But he didn't say anything." When he returned from his medical inspection his suspicions were confirmed. "I went up to the window and the con offered me a parcel. Then I was pushed through the door from behind. They closed the door and then all the cons in there set on me. Seven or eight of them altogether. They all looked hard cases. They didn't say anything at all; just started kicking at me until I went over and then they were kicking me in the face. They kicked these two teeth out in the front and fractured another one. They all got a few kicks in. And there was an officer outside the door who must have known what was going on. He was walking up to the door when I was pushed through it. He must have seen it. The next thing I really knew he opened the door and said 'Right, that's enough.' That must have been three or four minutes later. I don't know. It's very difficult to judge. I was standing there with blood pouring out of my mouth all over my clothes. He didn't say anything to them or do anything about it." Sometimes a co-operative staff absence is replaced by what appears to be an active staff participation."The governor asked me how it was that eight or nine men had got in my cell when I was supposed to be banged up. I didn't tell *him*, but I'll tell *you* how they got in. The officer came and opened the door and left it open. He walked away and eight or nine of them came in and kicked me over."

It would be perfectly possible to regard such accounts of collusion as isolated incidents arising from the sadistic or perverted nature of individual officers. A similar explanation could also be proposed for the violence inflicted on sex offenders by fellow inmates, but the number of incidents reported, their common format and the widespread involvement of other prisoners suggests that there is a social process at work and not just the feelings of a few puritanical offenders. The same applies, though in lesser measure, to the evidence about the part played by staff in the recruitment of Rule Forty Three men. There is, for instance, the reported attitude of the officer who opened the cell door: "He used to say openly that he hated Forty Threes and if he could, he'd make sure that we got into trouble. He said if he had his way, there'd be no Forty Threes. He'd kill them as they came in. He'd personally kick them to death."

For another man the unwelcome interest of a prison officer continued well past the period of reception: "On the way down here, I was supposed to stay at this prison overnight. I was there three days and I had a right time of it after the screw had paraded me all round the nick and told everybody what I was in for. In reception the screw said: 'Here he is, the dirty fucking sex case. Have a good look at him.' Then he marched me down past the kitchens. He said: 'Stand there lad.' And then he got half a dozen cons out of the kitchen and said: 'Look at this dirty fucking sex case.' He did that three times through the nick. When he put me in a cell he told all the cleaners the same and then fucked off and left the door open with eight cleaners lined up outside.'"[9]

The obverse face of staff involvement in the making of the Forty Threes is at first glance an overtly helpful one. A number of governors and officers had evidently gone out of their way to explain the dangers faced by a convicted sexual offender and to suggest that protection be sought. "When I went into prison on remand I went straight in front of the governor and he said: 'You're on Rule Forty Three.' No choice about it. He just put me straight on it. I hadn't even seen any prisoners, let alone them having a go at me. When I saw the Chief about it he said: 'It's in your own best interests. If the others get to know what you're in for they'll beat hell out of you.' He said he couldn't take any responsibility for what happened to me. I decided to stay on it."

It may be true that staff propose Rule Forty Three because they feel responsible for law and order within the institution. But except in the cases of men who are a physical danger to others, the application of the rule is a permissive one. In fact the responsibility of guarding a man on protection from the violent attentions of other prisoners is infinitely more burdensome than allowing him to take his chance on the wings or in the shops, and clearing up the mess if anything happens. Perhaps one of the reasons why officers spontaneously suggest Rule Forty Three to men who might otherwise survive in the ordinary prison environment, is the view held by many of them that sex offenders against children are incapable of fending for themselves if attacked. A note in one man's file, handwritten by a governor, summarises this staff sentiment: "He is a cowardly man and an easy target for bullies and sadists; there is a cult of persecuting the assaulters of children in this prison. Such intimidation is usually verbal and petty but it could lead to actual violence."

Instances of staff selection also occurred at Shepton Mallet itself when drafts arrived, as they sometimes did, containing a mixture of offenders, some bound for the protection wing, and some for the low security wing. If a man in the latter category happened to be a sex offender who had so far escaped the attention of his peers elsewhere, he was occasionally placed, willy nilly, on protection. "I came down here on a draft with three others and nobody was more surprised than me when they put me over here. I'd not had a moment's trouble with anyone; not whilst I was on remand, not at the other prison, not one bit. I couldn't go over to 'C' wing now; not after I've been here. I'm not going to complain." Whatever the reason for his previous immunity, the delicate fabric of this man's acceptance by other prisoners had now been damaged beyond hope of repair.

So, although prison officers seem to respond in opposite ways to newly received sex offenders, on the one hand aiding and abetting their persecution by other prisoners and on the other recommending to them immediate protective isolation, both responses have the same effect, which is that of adding to the growing ranks of the Rule Forty Three population.[10] Collaboration of this sort, which blurs the strict boundaries between the official and unofficial domains of the prison world, is far from a rarity. It occurs constantly, unstated and disavowed when necessary, but essential to the maintenance of equilibrium within the prison. Most of the collusion, however, takes place around 'instrumental' issues such as jobs or privileges, or in the form of a blind eye turned towards some illicit enterprise. What is interesting about staff participation in the scapegoating of sex offenders is that the issue is a purely 'expressive' one. If, as will be argued later, the attack on the 'sex pots' has something to do with inmate group cohesion, then staff involvement appears even less explicable.

Other Prisoners

The position of the sex offender who is detected in reception is obvious, but what happens to those who slip through the net? Perhaps the reception cons have not been presented with an opportunity to bring the provisions of Rule Forty Three forcibly to the attention of the prospective candidate. His colleague from court is not able to pass the word until the morning. The evening paper may be late or may have overlooked the case. The candidate may be atypically large or aggressive. But for those who survive the initial gauntlet of reception, the persecution is far from spent.

When the news leaks out, as it usually but not inevitably does, within a day or two, a week or two at most, then the game continues, but in a way which emphasises its collective nature. The basic arenas in which this part of the drama can be played out are the man's cell, the workshop, the exercise yard, the landings and the recesses.* Of these, the cell might be thought of as a private sanctuary, and the workshop and yard as falling directly under the control of the discipline staff. Traditionally, the landings and the recesses have been given over to the inmates, partly out of necessity, due to staff shortages, but also as part of a tacit ecological division of available territory. Lax supervision of the recess area permits its use by prisoners for settling personal scores or for visiting more organised forms of violence on those who have offended against the rules and norms of the inmate society. The workshop, and to a lesser extent the yard, are nominally official areas and less available for transactions of this sort. In the case of sex offenders, however, these constraints seem weaker, and something resembling an attitude of permission is often struck by staff, so that scapegoating frequently goes on in these public places quite unabated and with apparent impunity for those who take part in it. "Next day", said one man "they put me in the mail bag shop and they were all pointing at me and saying 'That's him, that's him.'"

Looking and pointing are both expressions of considerable hostility and their use in our society is controlled by an elaborate structure of expectations and prohibitions. Most basic of them is the injunction to children that it is rude to stare or to point. The making and breaking of eye contact, like elbow clutching rights, are hierarchically determined.[11] Their concerted use in a mass situation as an instrument of intimidation can be

*Recesses — lavatories, ablutions and slopping out places at the ends of landings.

extremely frightening for the recipients and deeply satisfying for the senders. "We all went into the Centre. It was about ten o'clock at night by then. They were all pointing at me and saying 'I'll get you.' I was terrified. It's a dreadful thing you know to have half the nick against you." Or from a written request for protection: "I saw all the men pointing me out, and about thirty of them got round the table in front of me."

For some men the fear induced by these or similar happenings is sufficient in itself to bring about an application for the Rule. That goal rather than physical retribution would seem, in fact, to be the desired end of much of the scapegoating activity. Pointing and naming as preliminaries also allow for the possibility that the wrong man has been selected, and for corrective action to be taken. If none is forthcoming, the accusation is held to be well founded; the adverse attention legitimated.

The chances of being on the receiving end of such attention are clearly increased by the seriousness of a man's sex offence, as measured by the length of sentence it attracted, or by the number of column inches devoted to it in the press. But many of the men who ended up at Shepton Mallet had been convicted of indecent assaults against children which did not involve the use of force. In a way, once the word has been passed that here is 'one of them' the details of what he has done seem to be of secondary importance. An anonymous note pushed under one man's cell door conveys the general message: 'You are in for interference to little boys or girls. It don't matter which. The first chance I get I will cut you bad. I've put the word about.' The same indifference to fine detail shows in other stories too. "When they opened me first morning a couple of cons came along and said 'You fucking bastard. You'd better get on Rule Forty Three or we'll break your fucking neck.' " Even a hint of solicitousness in a similar threat: "They shouted through the cell door: 'You'd better get on Rule Forty Three, they're going to get you.' " Or: "If you don't get on Rule Forty Three, we'll kick your face in". The nature of these generalities suggests that the response to sex offenders is not nicely calibrated to the awfulness of specific offences but has much more to do with the sealing of a status boundary within the prisoner community.

If the candidate does not yield at this stage, the campaign may be escalated. "The others in that cell, it was a six-cell, were after me as well. We used to eat our meals in there on a long wooden table and they used to say things about what I was in for. Call me names. Say I ought to be castrated, things like that. They were probably going to cut me up. I heard them planning to do something to me. I know there was a razor blade in there, hidden in the corner table. I was shaking like a leaf." But the creation of terror and the continued fulfillment of the Rule Forty Three role does not depend necessarily on face-to-face encounters. The isolation of the individual in a solitary cell and the transmission of threats, and occasionally more solid substances through the door, can unnerve the most self-possessed prisoner. Outside the door the collective nature of the activity continues, but with the Judas hole obscured to preserve the anonymity of the activists. Prisoners working as cleaners on the wing, like the 'trusties' in reception, are frequently to the fore in these proceedings. "The cleaners used to come and shout through the door; I'm sorry I've got to say this; they said: 'We're going to kick your balls in. We're going to cut your cock off.' " "They said how they were going to hang me or kick me to death." "They were going to kill me. They talked about scalding hot baths or hanging me." Even a novel version of the water torture was reported by one man. "And then the water came under the door. I don't suppose there was more than a jugful. But such was the state I was in I honestly thought they were going to keep on pouring water until it filled up the cell and drowned me."

For many of the men who have to endure recruitment to Rule Forty Three, threats and violence are unlikely to have been normal features of their former lives. To men who may never have been involved in fights as adults, both the prospect and the reality of personal aggression are unmanageable. Ethologists have described the ritualisation of aggressive behaviour in animals; in man the corresponding principle appears to be its formal organisation.[12] Personal violence tends to be acceptable only in highly institutionalised or consenting settings; wars, police exercises, judicial sentences, schools, sado-maso-chistic sexual encounters, boxing matches. What occurs outside of these arrangements is frowned upon, and for very large sections of the community, is virtually non-existent. Sex offenders against children tend to belong to this non-violent majority, a point presumably not lost on those in search of scapegoats. If the threat of violence does not produce the desired result of an application for protection, then the process moves inexorably towards a physical conclusion. Menacing gestures give way to throwing bits of dirt or trying to trip up the selected target, then spitting, kicking, and finally beatings, attempted drowning and attacks with knives or razors. "Six of them came for me in the recesses on the exercise. I kicked the first three and they ran off. And then the Paddy tried to get me with the razor. I'd kicked three and prodded another but I forgot the Brummie behind me. The Paddy told him to get hold of my arms and hold me while he cut me. He said: 'I know what you're in for. I don't like cunts like you'."[13] Curiously, graduates of these proceedings seemed to experience great difficulty in recalling what exactly was said to them. Their reluctance may be due to the generalised, abusive nature of the names and threats: 'dirty sex case' or 'you ought to be castrated'. But the accounts they gave of the actual violence shown to them are vivid and well described. It is of course possible that this selective recollection springs from an understandable unwillingness to incorporate such adverse labels into their own definitions of themselves.

Involuntary roles of great unattractiveness can usually only be sustained over time with the support of a strong peer culture or at a cost to the individual which borders on social annihila-tion, e.g. hereditary caste systems or the institutional treatment of the violent lunatic. Escape routes from such situations are rare. The one provided by the Rule Forty Three role is one which appears to reflect, mirror fashion, the relationship of the ordinary prisoner to society at large; that is as a visible absence. It is not sufficient in either of these situations; society to prisoner; prisoner to Forty Three, for the stigmatised simply to disappear. To be effective their absence calls for a continuing celebration. In the case of the prisoner *vis-à-vis* society these functions are served by the publicity surrounding court proceedings and by the highly visible walls of the prison. In the case of the Forty Threes they are provided by the public and participant nature of the proceedings which lead to protection, and by the maintenance of semi-public arrangements for the confinement of the solitary scapegoat in the punishment cells.[14]

A note submitted to a governor by a man seeking protection, puts into words this balance between presence and absence; between visibility and invisibility. 'Collective violence will hinder my entry into normal prison routine; I ask for *indefinite disassociation.*'

The Selection of Scapegoats

So far this account has not considered the reasons why one sex offender rather than another qualifies for the kind of treatment suffered by the men who ended up at Shepton Mallet. Clearly no more than a small minority of imprisoned sex offenders actually apply for protection, whatever the nature of their reception may have been. It would be easy to regard those who do as a purely random selection of men; a function of information fortuitously available within a given prison; or the chance presence of irascible and violent persecutors. There are, however, some clues to something more structured. Some of these are provided by sex offenders who escape detection during reception and who are left with a continuing problem of identity which they seek to solve by 'passing' for what they are not. To some extent they will be shielded in this enterprise by the prison etiquette which makes 'What are you in for?' an impertinent question. But if they are serving long sentences; they will find themselves fallen amongst thieves and robbers who are not only permitted, but positively expected to tell each other about their status inspiring activities outside. To remain silent in bull

sessions of that sort could well be dangerous, leading to
questions which demand answers with at least a hint of some
criminal interest or expertise about them. In one long term
prison, I once met a man who had been convicted of sexually
assaulting his own son, and was serving a sentence of eight
years alongside many murderers and robbers. He had quickly
become aware of the prevailing attitude towards his kind of
crime and had survived and found acceptance by fashioning
for himself a false identity of some complexity. To the extent
that he was still alive and well, it was also evidently of sufficient
credibility. The identity he adopted was that of a forger. He
had experience outside of the printing trade; knew a few words
and phrases that fitted his chosen metier; cultivated the acquain-
tance of known forgers, hesitantly at first, but with growing
confidence as he filled in the detail of a convincing criminal
autobiography. He even assumed the alien accents of South
London, which fitted his chosen image. Like the safe blower,
the forger is a lone craftsman and his lack of underworld connections were quite plausible. But he lived in fear, and because
of his personation, because of his 'passing', detection threatened
a double dose of retribution, first for the deceit on his fellows
and then for what he did originally. The extremity of his
situation irrupted in a bizarre way towards the end of his story
told with a constant eye on the open door of his cell, alert to
callers or listeners on the landing. 'Down there', he said, pointing
towards the ground floor where the punishment and protection
cells stood along the 'ones', 'There's a bloke that cut open his
little girl to get into her. Cut her open with a razor. If I get at
the bastard I'll kill him. I'll kill him.'

This man's simulated biography worked because it was not
challenged, but for men in his situation, the danger is always
present, as the case of a man on the non-protection wing at
Shepton showed. Some of the prisoners there had themselves
been convicted of sexual offences but had escaped positive
recruitment to the Rule at their prisons of reception. One such
man, who will be called Kegworth, arrived at Shepton Mallet
from another western prison, and having negotiated reception

without mishap was located on the non-protection wing. After a time there arrived from the same prison another man called Burden, who had been employed on the cleaning party there and had played a leading part in attempts to stigmatise Kegworth shortly after his conviction for offences of indecent assault on young girls. 'He told me he was in for nicking motor cars but I soon told him what I thought of him. I told him he was a dirty animal and he ought to be doctored' said cleaner Burden.

Kegworth remembered him well. "He was a cleaner over there and one day he came outside my cell and read out the bit in the paper; read it through the hole. He said 'Listen to this, you dirty bastard' and then read it out. Then he got three of his mates to come for me in the bog." Like the bogus forger he lived in constant fear. "Every time there's a draft comes in, I'm shitting bricks in case there's someone who knows. I go in for dinner when there's a new lot of receptions and I'm white with fear that there's going to be someone there." One day there was; his former accuser Burden, who described what happened. "When I got here, I walked on the wing and the first person I saw was Kegworth. Christ, he went as white as a sheet when I saw him. He was afraid I'd tell people what he was in for."

Burden never did tell anyone, something which he chose to explain in terms of altruism. "I thought, well, it's not up to me to make it any more difficult for him. He's doing his punishment — that's enough for him." But a more likely explanation, according to Kegworth, was the fact that: "It's different here. I'm like top of the heap here. There are a few of us, like a click (clique) and we just get what we want." The protection he derived from membership of this high status group also carried a cost to be counted in terms of anxiety; a situation observed by the cleaner with some irony; "I used to watch him with them sometimes, laughing and joking, and I used to think 'Ha, if you only knew what he was in for you wouldn't be so keen'." Kegworth himself saw the irony, but little hope of pity. "It'd be worse for me because I'm their friend now. I'm at the top. They've eaten with me, worked with me, played darts with me and then to find out, they'd kill me."

Also like the forger he had to come to terms with the views his new-found friends expressed about his unadmitted self. "They talk about what they'd like to do to people like that. They ought to shoot 'em or cut their bollocks off. I keep quiet about it."

It is possible that large and physically adept men like Keg-worth may be more able to escape scapegoating. But a repeated theme in the accounts of violence given by the men who succumbed to it was that the attackers invariably came many handed, thus neutralising any natural physical advantages they might possess. "One at a time I could manage them, but not six. I asked the governor if he would let them into my cell one at a time but he wouldn't."

A quite different possibility is that the person singled out for special attention is of peculiar of particularly obnoxious appearance. It has been proposed by Corsini that offenders of different types can be ranked in order of physical attractiveness; and that face-to-face offenders will be more attractive than more furtive ones. He suggests for example that robbers will be more handsome than burglars and that rapists in turn will be better looking than indecent assaulters.[15] Prison officers at Shepton sometimes claimed that Rule Forty Three men did not look normal. An objective test of the proposition was beyond the scope of this study, but the only measure of physique uniformly available for the Shepton and general prison populations, that of height, showed no significant difference. Amongst the men interviewed, it is true, there were individuals who felt themselves to be ugly: "The officers are always having a go at me. Saying that I'm fat or I'm ugly." Or the following conversation:

"What would really settle me down is a good steady girl friend."

"Yes."

"But what chance have I got?"

"What do you mean?"

"With a face like this."

"Like what?"

"Ugly, broken nose. Half me teeth missing. Girls say to me

go away Frankenstein'. That hurts sometimes."

Ordinary prisoners, for their part, are not particularly explicit about the reasons for their violent treatment of potential Forty Threes. One man who operated on the fringes of big time organized crime, put it this way: "They're like animals. I've got to live with them. See them when I'm having my breakfast. They want exterminating."

Burden, the cleaner at another western prison, gave a fuller account of his part in the scapegoating of Rule Forty Threes there, and of the attitudes he brought to the job; "I had a very good job there, in the trials and remands. I was trusted. I had the run of the place. We got some very nasty cases brought in there. I used to know all about them from reading the *Echo*. Not because I wanted to know about them, but it's my local paper. One of them had cut open his daughter to have intercourse with her. And he only got probation. And I'm here for two and a half years for doing damage to a silly little piece of glass that's not worth more than thirty shillings. It's not fucking right."

An apocryphal and often mentioned figure with a razor makes an appearance in Burden's comments at this point, and in a way which suggests the existence of an additional technique of 'neutralisation' to those nominated by Sykes and Matza in their typology.[16] It is one which rests on an appeal to relativity; 'At least I don't go round raping little girls; cutting them open with razors; buggering small boys; fiddling in a dirty way with other people's innocent children.' Rather than condemning the condemners, this kind of neutralisation reflects or 'refracts' criticism onto offenders whose behaviour is such that *everyone* can agree to condemn it. And it makes an additional appeal; an appeal which no doubt lends strength to the fury of the attacks which other prisoners make on sexual offenders. It is an appeal to family loyalties and to the naturally protective feelings of fathers which are outraged by the mere thought of their children being sexually abused. And the fact that they are in prison and impotent to fulfill this protective function for their own children adds an ironic edge to the cause of their anger. Burden the cleaner, spoke for many prisoners when he described a man who had enticed girls into situations where he could sexually assault them, as: 'Just an animal. I've got daughters of my own and if it had been one of them. It might have been my daughter.' There is of course nothing unexpected about these statements and these kinds of sentiments, but in the exceptional atmosphere of prison society, they fuel the process of justifying the scapegoating of sexual offenders by exaggerating or distorting the nature of their offence behaviour.

Horrific though some of the offences committed by Forty Three men at Shepton actually were, the reality was embroidered and embellished by the non-Forty Threes into realms of fantasy, as in this tale told by a thief on 'C' wing. "One man over there was working for the council doing some painting work at this house and the women had to go out for a few minutes. She left her baby in its pram, her eighteen month old baby, and went, off. While she was gone this man went and put his penis in the child's mouth. The child thought it was a dummy." At the time there was no prisoner on the protection wing whose offence fitted this description in even the remotest way, but it confirms the development of stereotypes about Forty Threes, even at Shepton Mallet where the two wings were in theory totally segregated.

Taken together, then, the experiences of men who applied for the protection of Rule Forty Three because of the nature of their offences, confirms the existence of a social process in which some of the salient values and structures of the inmate subculture of the English prison system are to be seen. The distinctive roles of the reception cons and the cleaners in the scapegoating emerge quite clearly, as does the collaborative part played by some officers in the proceedings. Patterns of collective action, some of them culminating in violence, are evident, reflecting a commitment to shared values and an active involvement by large numbers of ordinary prisoners. These activities draw some of their vitality from, and in turn contribute to the reinforcement of stereotypes about sex offenders, which are then further sustained by the socially visible arrangements made for their solitary confinement under the provisions of Rule Forty Three.

Many of these features occur in the following account of recruitment to Rule Forty Three given by a fifty-year old catering worker serving a twelve months sentence for indecent assault on boys:

"When we got into reception the first thing the screw does is to throw my record down to the con who's sat there in reception. He was sat at the table with his feet sprawled out and smoking big cigarettes. Him and his buddies, they run the place.

"So he looks in the record and reads all through it. 'Christ', he says. 'What have we got here and then he starts calling me names, all filthy names, you know, 'fucking this' and 'fucking that'. He was a real rough type of bloke, a Londoner, always looking for a scrap.

"Then the screw came and he said: 'Fucking get round there and get your fucking clothes off.' They bundled 'em all into a cardboard box anyhow and bunged the lid on. I said 'Look out, that's a fucking new suit' and they laughed and said 'Don't worry about that.' I had a bath and they gave me all old, dirty clothes to wear and size eleven shoes. I take eight's. Then they put me in a reception cell and brought me supper and that was that.

"The number one cleaner, he was a funny bloke. When I was coming out of the cell, he said 'What are you in for?' I thought quick and said 'Robbery.' 'You fucking liar,' he said. 'I know what you're in for.' Then he started with all the dirty names, you know what they are. There was a big crowd of them all about then.

"First thing that happened next morning was I was brought in front of a PO (Principal Officer) and a chaplain. The PO told me to go on Rule Forty Three. 'It's all round the prison what you're in for', he said. 'It's for your own good. Don't go in the shop; go behind your door.' I told him I might as well go in the shop. 'It's all controlled in there, there's the officers, nothing can happen.'

"So I went in the bag shop and they all started pointing at

me and shaking their fists. I sat down at the front and straight away there were three or four of them round me calling me a dirty bastard and kicking me. Roughnecks, the sort that like trouble. I tried to clear them away with my arms but that just made it worse. It went on all morning like that. When it was exercise the screw said: 'All wash your hands.' I thought 'Well I'm not going into the corner because they'll fucking kill me.' I hung back but the screw said 'Go and get your fucking hands washed.' When I got there they all got round me, fifteen or twenty of them, shouting at me. And they were hitting me and kicking me between the legs. One of them kicked me in the rupture and that caused me a lot of pain. If that had busted I would have copped me lot.

"There were three screws there and they didn't take a blind bit of notice; pretended they couldn't hear anything. One of them was filling in the work book by the door and the other two pretended to be doing things.

"When we got out onto exercise I went up to the PO in charge and said I wasn't going to walk round with the others because I'd get killed. He said 'Fucking get in there.' I said: 'Well I can't. I want to see the governor.' 'Get back on fucking exercise.' So I refused and he said 'Well stand there then.' As they all came past they were gobbing on me and taking kicks at me. The PO never tried to stop them.

"On the wing you queue up for governor's and it was just as bad there. They were still attacking me. The screw wouldn't let me get out of the line. He made me stand there until my turn.

"I went down on Forty Three. I've never complained about it to anyone. Could you do anything about it? Could you try to get it stopped? You could use your influence. I can't do anything."

Non-Sex Offenders

But all of this applies only to the 'nature of offence' men who constituted two-thirds of the Shepton group, and it remains to consider the experience of the others; the so-called 'grasses' or informers. The governor of Manchester Prison had reported to the Home Office at the end of 1965 a clear-cut division of his Rule Forty Three inmates into three groups:

1. Nature of offence, 40%
2. Informers, 35%
3. Debtors, 25%[16]

The policy pursued at Manchester was to encourage 'voluntary repatriation' of Rule Forty Three cases. If they could be so persuaded, the men were returned to ordinary location, either at the prison from which they came, or in another where they were less likely to be known. The governor went on to say that successful relocations consisted almost entirely of informers and debtors and that sex offenders were unlikely ever to request return to normal conditions. It was his recommendation that separate facilities for Rule Forty Three should be reserved for that category of man. The Shepton population which had been constructed on the remnant of the Manchester one contained, therefore, significantly lower proportions of the last two categories, 'grasses' and debtors. And before detailed study of the relevant individuals it was not possible to allocate non-sex offenders to either group with any certainty.

They proved, on examination, to form a highly heterogeneous group, and during two complete years' work at the prison only one man ever proved willing to embrace, unasked, the unqualified title of 'grass'.[17] The recorded fact of a sex offence, by contrast, and particularly where it has led to Forty Three status, is virtually inescapable. The offence behaviour itself is, however, irrelevant to the everyday life of the prison community and is odious only in relation to the 'expressive' part of the informal code. 'Grasses' have, by definition, been involved in the workings of the inmate culture; hence their access to information which they are alleged to have transmitted to some official person. Betrayal merits a more vindictive response because it endangers the livelihood and liberty of others who are engaged in illicit enterprises. The 'grass', therefore, can go quite literally in fear for his life. On that score alone a man might be forgiven for devising in retrospect a revised version of his application for Rule Forty Three protection. Add to it the status implications of being a 'grass' and the label becomes even more unacceptable. Hence the almost unbroken record of disavowal amongst the non-sex men.

And since Rule Forty Three recruits along the margins of human behaviour in an extreme social situation, it would also be remarkable if it did not attract a proportion of prisoners in pursuit of essentially private strategies; some of them intelligible; others less so. In the latter category were men who said things which sounded almost like parodies of the symptoms of paranoid schizophrenia: "I came here to get away from the voices. But it's no good. They're just outside the gate here. They follow me about. They've got an agreement with the Home Secretary that they can have me when I go out. They'll probably kill me." "I heard a noise like they were busy sharpening knives and I knew that it was for me." Some of these men, with or without such clear-cut psychiatric symptoms, continued to refuse association with others even at Shepton, where everyone else in the wing had shared a common experience in other prisons. They remained behind their doors and nothing would induce them to come out. One or two displayed other manifestations of disturbance such as eating glass salt cellars, or engaging in spectacular suicide attempts.

Two further kinds of private strategy were those of attempting to reach desired destinations within the prison system, and something which might be called 'subcultural resignation'. A few men claimed that they were using the provisions of the Rule to achieve a change of prison after more straightforward methods had failed. The cost of employing Rule Forty Three as a travel ticket is, however, high. The front cover of a protection case record is marked to that effect, and in any case a stay at Shepton would be recorded somewhere on the file cover, indelibly and for all time. A Dartmoor man had been warned of this by an officer: "Well, I thought about it and I thought; 'Well I'm not coming back.' So I sort of burned my bridges." It was also something which concerned men on the non-Forty Three wing; that they would be marked by stigma simply through having been at Shepton.

'Subcultural resignations' seem to arise from the similarity of treatment which is meted out in long-term prisons to men on punishment and those on protection. Cells for both purposes are usually located together to make surveillance easier and to isolate their occupants from the possibility of contact with other inmates. Punishment cells, usually a row of a dozen or so on one of the lower landings, but often still referred to as 'the chokey block', represent the official culture's attempt to create a prison within a prison; a sanction for the myriad rules and orders which in theory keep the 'nick' quiet. Rule Forty Three is an informal version of this prison within a prison for the inmate subculture. Both the 'chokey' and the segregation cells define and illustrate the presence of the deviants they contain and thereby the deviance they seek to constrain. If a man finds that he is spending a great deal of time in the 'chokey' cells because of rule infringements or because of a feud with a particular officer, then protection may eventually appear preferable to punishment. The net effects on his daily round are practically nil, but as a Forty Three he has been seen to exercise at least some kind of choice. And his choice means that opportunities for rule breaking or for being picked on have been reduced to vanishing point. Two or three men of this type claimed that their standing with peers at Parkhurst or Dartmoor was still good and that they could return to normal association any time they chose, but it is doubtful that they would be accepted back in any other than a most qualified way. At all events none of them ever did apply for relocation from Shepton Mallet.

Explanations offered by men in this group for being on the Rule include suggestions that they were on 'governor's Forty Three', placed there because of the grave physical danger which they represented to other prisoners and staff. In none of these cases did the facts seem to tally with their claims, and the official files made no mention of what would have been major security matters. Personal grudges, sometimes arising from bent enterprises gone wrong and sometimes from strictly private situations, were also reported. The man who hit his companion in minor crime over the head and ran off with the day's takings, for instance, took refuge against the righteous indignation of his former colleague who followed him into prison. Living with someone else's wife or girl whilst he is in prison has also been known to provoke violent reprisals when both parties have found themselves subsequently serving a sentence together.

In a small number of cases it is possible to glimpse the working of the criminal underworld. "I was in London, on accumulated visits and they sent this geezer in to see me, didn't they? Like he was from the Krays. He was one of their boys. They wanted me to bring money in and a gun. I told them I wanted no part of it, not guns. They said: 'Well you will do it, because if you don't your people outside will get hurt.' It was all friendly, smiles and all that, but they meant it. I've known people it's been done to." The logic of all that is straightforward and so is the language. Compared with the reported speech of the sex offenders there are the clear accents of the criminal subculture beyond the walls. The pursuit of the 'grass' is also something that proceeds across the prison wall and casts a shadow over his life no matter where he is. "I've had a tooth out and a couple of cuts from them, but nothing serious" said one man. "The first time they got me was in Oxford Street. Two of them, very smart fellers in suits, got hold of me and tried to take me round the back somewhere where their mates were. It didn't matter where I went they always followed me."

Any effective system of sanctions, even that of the criminal subculture, rests on two factors; certainty and, if possible, swiftness. "When I got into the prison, there they were. Half a dozen of them. First night I got a kicking. When the screw unlocked the door four of them came in and gave me a kicking."

In each of these three instances there was involvement in organised crime and some breach of the norms of its subculture; refusal to aid an escape attempt; running off with the loot; and giving evidence in court which the gang, if not the informant, had defined as harmful to their cause.

Only two men admitted that tobacco debts to prison barons

were the cause of their application for Rule Forty Three. Only two instances amongst so many men might suggest that tobacco baroning in ordinary prisons is less important than it is some-times made out to be. But there is an alternative explanation for the dearth of tobacco debtors amongst the Forty Threes which emerges from the case of the man who had borrowed 'snout' against bad debts and soon found, at compound rates of interest, that he owed the barons more than eight ounces: "I couldn't pay back eight ounces and I didn't know anyone outside who could buy it off for me. One day I came out of my cell and there was one of the mob coming for me along the landing. I went the other way and there was one there as well. So I jumped over the railings and swung down onto the floor. I went into the office and went on Forty Three. When I was down there (on the block) they came to the door. They said if I came off, and went down the bath house and took a medium kicking that would be quits. I didn't fancy that so I stayed where I was."

The threats made towards this man were not designed to serve the same purpose as those directed towards sex offenders. Their aim was not so much to fill the Forty Three cells as to restore a state of equilibrium within the unofficial economy. A debtor undealt with in a small-scale society is a direct threat to the whole basis of the informal system for overcoming the pains of imprisonment. The 'barons' set their 'mob' to work. The pro-tection of Rule Forty Three thwarts the intended demonstration of sanctions in action. They offer a 'medium' kicking as an inducement to come out, and in exchange for expungement of the debt. In other words, a semblance of punishment will serve to impress the real message on other potential debtors. Enhanced in the telling, episodes like this reinforce the rule of the economic bosses and they are presumably prepared to write off considerable losses as the price of maintaining their positions. And no doubt they will sometimes find men willing to submit to a kicking rather than face prison-lifelong exile from their fellows. A punitive beating, once over, restores the balance; Rule Forty Three, like the albatross, lingers on for ever. Few men sufficiently engaged in the informal culture to patronise the bookie or the baron will willingly forgo the regard of their peers. The principle of reciprocity is stronger than fear of reprisal. And the difference in kind between these economic sanctions and the kickings bestowed on 'sexpots' is that the former are meant to be essentially restorative in effect.

Selection methods for Rule Forty Three, whether by staff or inmates, for sex offences or for 'grassing', were originally designed to translate the candidate to a state of solitary confinement and to maintain him there, visibly apart. Because of the growing numbers involved and the destructive effect on the individual of prolonged confinement in these conditions, the Home Office had decided to congregate Forty Threes, first at Manchester, and subsequently at Shepton, so that they might enjoy a measure of association with their peers without fear of personal violence. The recruitment routes discussed here define the characteristics of the population at Shepton and imply some of the features of the social system which they might be expected to construct. The next chapter describes in more detail some of the characteristics of the individual Rule Forty Three men at Shepton Mallet as a prelude to looking at how they combined to form a prison society of their own; the community of scapegoats.

Notes

1. T. Mathiesen, The Sociology of Prisons — Problems for further research, *British Journal of Sociology* 17, 1966 has also drawn attention to the absence of any serious work on the relations of the prison to its social environment. Entry and departure across the boundary of the 'total institution' are obvious topics for specific studies. Generic discussions of induction or degradation ceremonies do not fill this gap. Elliot Studt, however, has used the concept of status passage in a useful discussion of the parole process and the difficulties it poses for the parolee. *The Re-entry of the Offender into the Community*, Office of Juvenile Delinquency and Youth Development, U.S. Dept. of Health, Education and Welfare, 1967.

2. Degradation ceremonies, either singly or in sequence, aim to be:
   (a) comprehensive in their effect on the various identities and roles of the subject;

(b) retrospective in their annihilation of integrity. See H. Garfinkel, Conditions of Successful Degradation Ceremonies, *American Journal of Sociology*, 61, 1956. It follows that when successfully applied they are also predictive both of self-conception by the subject and of responses by others.

3. E.g. Gresham M. Sykes, *The Society of Captives*, A Study of a Maximum Security Prison, Princeton University Press, 1958.
Richard A. Cloward, Social Control in the Prison, in *Theoretical Studies in the Social Organization of the Prison*, Social Science Research Council, Pamphlet 15, 1960.

4. Wherever boundaries confine some social situation or system there will be guardians to prevent unauthorised 'passing' in or out, and in more structural settings there will be special arrangements for getting in or out. These are gateways manned by specialists who control the quality of the intakes and the outputs. Bus conductors, examining bodies, secretaries, madames in brothels, are all examples of the function.

5. T. Morris and P. Morris, *Pentonville*, A sociological study of a prison, *op. cit.*

6. At the time of this study the prison grapevine was filled with rumours about the escape from Dartmoor of Frank Mitchell. Details about his disappearance were in circulation long before they featured in police evidence at a subsequent trial, when it was alleged, but not proved, that he had been shot and encased in a concrete pillar supporting an urban motorway.

7. Gresham M. Sykes and David Matza, Techniques of Neutralisation. A Theory of Delinquency, *American Sociological Review* 22, 1957.

8. The accounts collected for this part of the study were freely given by prisoners on protection in the course of what appeared to them to be general conversation about their experiences in other prisons. Since they were not aware that the information was being collected for any particular purpose it is unlikely that they engaged in deliberate distortion. It must be acknowledged that no check was possible on the accuracy of what individual men said, but the consistency of the whole set of interviews indicates that the general picture presented here is not too far from the truth.

9. These events bear a family likeness to the treatment of individual prisoners of war by the North American Indian tribe of the Huron. The tethered captive, usually an Iroquois, was led from village to village as visibly as possible and with maximum opportunity for the citizens to participate physically and fully in the scapegoating process. The torments of each gauntlet were designed not to threaten the survival of the prisoner, which was essential for his final lingering death in a collective orgy of torture. Significantly these blood-stained boundaries encompassed a cohesive and gentle culture, with few defined categories of crime. See Bruce G. Trigger, *The Huron, Farmers of the North*, Holt Rinehart & Winston, N.Y., 1969.

10. Two other men reported trouble where they might least have expected it; in prison hospitals. At an establishment elsewhere, whilst on Rule

Forty Three, a sex offender had attempted to kill himself. He had been sent to the 'hospital' for 'psychiatric observation.' "When I got there one of the officers said 'I've been on the lookout for this feller. I'll take him up.' They took me up and put me in a strip cell. And they put a jacket on me, not a strait jacket, but it had big buckles on it here at the neck and the back. The officers pushed me in and started pushing me about; two of them. Calling me a 'fucking bastard' and all like that." And an informer recounted the following experience: "I was in the hospital to have a gall-stone removed. Nobody bothered me except two officers who knocked me about because I was a Forty Three. I was lying in bed with the stitches. They had to lift me out of bed to change it. An officer came in and told me to fold the sheets and put them outside the door. Well, I struggled up and got them folded and put them outside. Then the other screw came up and threw them back inside. He got hold of me and smacked me round the face and threw me against the radiator. He said 'We don't like Forty Threes here.' That night my stitches burst and I got a stitch abscess. I was in agony."

11. Erving Goffman, *Behavior in Public Places*, Free Press of Glencoe, 1963.

12. Konrad Lorenz, *On Aggression*, Methuen, London, 1966.

13. Only a minority of the men on Rule Forty Three had experienced actual violence at the hands of other prisoners, but of those who did, a remarkably high proportion mentioned that their aggressors were Scots, Irish or Welsh. The Celtic fringes have a reputation for 'wild men' and there may be a similar prison stereotype. Alternatively, one of the few distinguishing marks left to a man in prison is his regional accent plus an accompanying label, 'Jock', 'Mick' or 'Taff'. Such men would therefore be more readily identified by the victims.

14. As with officers, the disappearance of a man 'behind his door' may not deter other inmates from continuing their cruel ministrations. One man told me that in another prison, the Forty Three in the next cell passed to him a piece of paper on which he had placed all the fragments of ground glass which he was able to extract from his dinner one day.

15. Raymond J. Corsini, Appearance and Criminality, *American Journal of Sociology*, 65, 1949.

16. Home Office, *Report on the work of the Prison Department 1965*, HMSO, Cmnd. 3088, 1966.

17. Due to the notoriety of his case he was unable to do otherwise.

CHAPTER 3

One Hundred Forty Threes

Who were the men who were recruited from the general prison population by the processes described in the last chapter? We have seen that they fell into two principal groups: offenders against children, mostly sexual but with some violence cases; and a mixed bag of non-sex offenders containing informers, debtors and mentally disturbed men. The purpose of this chapter is to describe in more detail the members of each of these groups; firstly in order to see whether their combined characteristics throw any further light on the processes of scapegoating of which they are the collective product; and secondly to look for some indications of the kind of society they might be expected to form amongst themselves.

The daily protection population at Shepton Mallet fluctuated around the eighty mark, and information was collected on all the men who were in residence on 1 January 1968 together with every consecutive admission subsequently up to a total of one hundred. Information was taken from the official prison records on each of these men, and from the files held in the welfare office. This included data from the Initial Index Card, a summary description held separately from the files, Criminal Record Office lists of previous convictions and sentences, plus police antecedent reports, and any medical or probation reports submitted to courts. In addition, since most of the records were silent on the subject, requests were sent to investigating police authorities for more detailed descriptions of the sexual or violent offences committed by the men.[1]

The offences for which these one hundred men were convicted and serving sentences of imprisonment are shown in Table 3.1.

Table 3.1 Type of offence

Offences against children				Property	Violence	Rape	Total
Sexual offences			Violence against own children				
female victims		male victims					
other children	own children						
17	14	27	6	30	5	1	100

Sixty-four men had been convicted of offences against children, either sex, fifty-eight cases; or violence, six; a further thirty were imprisoned for a variety of property offences; five had committed violence against adults, and one had raped an adult woman.

The offenders against children have been subdivided in the table into those who committed acts of violence against their own children, and sexual offenders, some of whom were involved with their own daughters, some with unrelated girls, and some with unrelated boys. Pedophile offenders are ordinarily quite specific in their sexual preferences, but six of the fifty-eight were serving sentences imposed on them for offences against both boys and girls. They have been allocated to either the 'male' or the 'female' category according to the sex of the victim in the most serious charge or in the majority of the offences alleged against them. Girl victims present another dimension as well; that of age, since the nearer they are to age of consent the less likely it is that other prisoners will take exception to offences against them. Prison lore has it that, providing the age range is roughly right, then appearance is what matters, not legal age, and that there is no such thing as rape. 'Rape' is held to be something which a woman cries afterwards; a belated expression of regret that she gave way, or an attempt to redefine what went on so as to support assertions of innocence or fidelity. Garbled versions were to be heard at Shepton of Clarence Darrow's fabled court room demonstration with quill and inkwell that permission is necessary for penetration.

Family Offenders

Offences within the family involve both sex and violence, but since the characteristics of the offending fathers seem to fall into common patterns they will be dealt with together. Fourteen cases involved sexual activity between fathers and daughters, but the actual charges brought against them were incest and attempted incest (six cases), unlawful sexual intercourse (two) and a collection of indecent assaults and multiple offence charges (six cases) which included buggery and attempted buggery.

There were six men convicted of violence against their own children, in four instances leading to the death of a child, but none of them had been convicted of murder (two cases of manslaughter, one grievous bodily harm, and one child neglect). In the other two cases where death did not result, but only broken bones and brain damage, the men had been charged with, and found guilty of, neglect and grievous bodily harm respectively.

Three types can be tentatively distinguished from the known details of these family offenders' out-of-prison lives, the 'respectable' (five), the 'disorganised' (ten) and the 'disturbed' (five).

'Respectable'

'Respectable' offenders lead normally law-abiding lives, have reasonable or good work records and small families. Their offences appear to arise out of situational tensions or opportunities; a father left alone to cope with crying children; a sudden flaring of the temper; panic efforts to undo the damage which make it worse; a sexually withdrawn or absent wife; the presence of a daughter. Of course these are far from uncommon conjunctions of situation and opportunity and it is not possible with so few instances even to begin to understand why some men succumb to such impulses, whilst others do not. Nor is it possible to determine how these particular cases came to official notice when many others clearly escape detection. But the offences do stand out as singular and exceptional events in otherwise respectable lives. For example:

CASE ONE. A twenty-seven-year-old transit clerk with an impeccable work record, moderate personal habits and described as 'an excellent husband and father' apparently lost his temper whilst attempting to pacify his six-month-old daughter and struck her in the face. In the course of desperate and vain attempts to stem the subsequent bleeding the child was suffocated.

Two years for grievous bodily harm.

CASE TWO. A twenty-four-year-old lorry driver, deserted by his wife and left to look after a six-year-old daughter engaged in sexual activities with her amounting to incest. It is difficult to believe that a full act of intercourse can have taken place, but precise detail was not available in the record.

Six years for incest.

Incest and infanticide evoke extreme degrees of moral and aesthetic revulsion in our culture, and anthropologically speaking parent—child incest is the subject of a more universally expressed taboo than any other single item of human behaviour.[2] 'Respectable' offenders are not insensitive to these moral and social pressures, and they alone amongst the Forty Threes were prone to volunteer without prompting expressions of remorse and contrition about their offences. A few of them appeared almost to welcome the swingeing sentences they had received; "I know it's a long time but I know I've got to pay for what I did. I just want to get it done and then I can start again." They exhibit, in fact, just those attitudes which the system, the court and the prison expects of the 'ideal' convicted person, a rational acceptance of guilt and a willing resignation to the longueurs of imprisonment. 'Model' prisoners of this kind participate in a reciprocal strengthening of the moral order. Their attitudes confirm the 'straight' culture, both in and out of prison.

'Disorganised'

'Disorganised' family offenders present a contrary picture;

one of large families, prolonged or permanent unemployment, poverty, ill health and histories of petty offences and minor violence; the classic symptoms of the 'multi-problem family', in fact. Roles played by the fathers in families of this sort seem to be of two kinds. There are those who rule their broods with rods of iron; rigid, demanding men seemingly made worse by their incapacities in other directions; and there are some hopeless, collapsed individuals for whom even the word 'inadequate' sounds somehow too positive.

CASE THREE. A thirty-two-year-old Scots labourer married to a part-time prostitute in poor health. Five children in the family, two of them by other fathers. Approved school, Borstal and many prison sentences for petty offences. Persistently ill treated his children, particularly when drunk, beating them, kicking them, and in the case for which he was tried, breaking one child's bones extensively.

Four years for cruelty and neglect.

CASE FOUR. A forty-five-year-old labourer with a long history of unemployment, a tubercular wife, eight children and a diagnosed anxiety neurosis. Over a period of years he seduced each of his daughters as they reached puberty, and protected them as far as he could from the attentions of more youthful suitors. In this case, and it was not unique, the sexual behaviour between father and daughters was known to the wife and mother of the family, who apparently used the knowledge as a lever on his behaviour in other respects, by threatening to tell the police if he did not comply with her wishes.

Three years for incest.

Although the word 'disorganised' has been used to characterise this type of family, it need not be taken to imply a total lack of cohesion or of long-term loyalties. Incestuous fathers can and do return to their families after serving long sentences. On occasions they even resume the offending relationship. The marriages of these men, during their tenure of the Rule Forty Three role, were of variable quality. Some had been broken before the offence, some were broken by it. Some continued unaffected and yet others were plagued by mutually violent feelings and hysterical correspondence. But communication, whether good, bad or non-existent, is a poor guide to the true state of matrimonial affairs. The wife of one Forty Three man had not written or received letters from her husband during the whole of the six years he served of a previous ten-year sentence, but she received him back at the end of it, and they lived in apparent harmony until a further fifteen-year sentence took him from her again.

'Disturbed'

The 'disturbed' group contains a small number of individuals with histories of psychiatric hospitalisation, or whose demeanour during or after their offences indicated some degree of mental disturbance. Since they are only five in number they do not have many other characteristics in common. One had been a prisoner of war and spent many years subsequently in mental hospitals. Another rationalised his extensive sexual activities in religious terms. He had been fulfilling God's will. He had literally visited the sins of the fathers upon the children.

Extreme religiosity is a recurring feature of life amongst the Forty Threes and will be examined in more detail later, but its focus is usually on forgiveness and future conduct more than on retrospective justification.[3] Two cases have been placed in this group because of the extreme degrees of apathy or indifference they showed to the consequences of their actions. The family patterns and previous histories of the 'disturbed' do not appear also to be 'disorganised' and only one of them had any previous conviction for dishonesty.

Female Victim Offenders

Seventeen men had been convicted of sexual offences against female children who were not members of their immediate family. Their actual convictions were: indecent assault, nine cases; unlawful sexual intercourse, four; rape and attempted rape and buggery, four cases. All the girls were aged between four and fourteen. The clearest division of cases that can be made in this group is between those where the offender and the victim were previously known to each other, and those where they were not. Known victim cases, of which there were nine, will be referred to as 'situational' ones, and the eight unknown victim ones as the 'random'.

'Situational'

'Situational' offences are those which arise out of existing relationships within a relatively settled context such as a cohabitation or a permanent lodging. Victims tend then to be the children of relatives, neighbours, friends and landladies. They do not take fright at the first steps in a game which must appear to them indistinguishable from an ordinary interest or affection. As events escalate from romping and petting to fondling, and finally to the putting together of penis and private parts, with or without some attempt at penetration, there comes a point at which discovery is practically bound to occur. That point may be reached with the infliction of physical pain or when there is accidental disclosure; a childish remark; a returning mother who interrupts an attempt at intercourse.

In five of the nine 'situational' cases the victims were girls in their early teens who had participated in the 'offences' over quite long periods of time. Even younger girls too were sometimes referred to by the offenders as willing participants. A relationship described by one man in terms of companionship, tenderness and affection, *and* sex, possessed all the attributes of a proper love affair. The only inappropriate thing about it was that he was forty-two years old and she was eleven. In cases like this it is the age gap between the participants rather than what they actually do with each other which causes dismay and anger in others. Much of the reported behaviour in these mens' offences resembles the mutual sexual exploration engaged in by children which, if it is discovered, is typically discouraged, but not normally dealt with in the framework of the criminal law. Force was reported to have been used on a girl in only one of the 'situational' offences.

CASE FIVE. A forty-one-year-old labourer with three previous convictions for violent sex assaults on girls, including the rape of his own daughter, took lodgings with a family having a nine-year-old daughter. Over a period of time he made progressive and non-violent sexual contacts with the girl, which did not come to light until he was disturbed in a rather more forceful attempt at intercourse with her ten-year-old cousin, who had called at the house when both mother and daughter were out. For three such offences he was sentenced to ten years imprisonment.

It is difficult to make any estimate of the discomfort suffered by any of the victims of 'situational' offenders, but tragic outcomes are possible even when physical pain is not inflicted.

CASE SIX. A thirty-one-year-old labourer from South London went to live with a friend and his family. After an argument the friend left home leaving the labourer in the house. He moved into the matrimonial bed and also had regular sexual intercourse with the twelve-year-old daughter who slept in the same room and who was alleged to be already promiscuous. Immediately before his trial on charges of unlawful sexual intercourse with her, the girl committed suicide by gassing herself. She may have been pregnant.

Two years for unlawful sexual intercourse.

'Random'

Amongst the 'random' group, men who assault unknown female victims, there occur those extremes of behaviour which the assailants of the Forty Threes are wont to ascribe to all of them. Four of the nine men who picked on random victims were actually charged with rape or attempted rape.

One part of society's response to deviance is an attempt to come to terms with the general problem of unmerited or unjustified suffering. When rich corporations are cheated of their resources by working-class youths or when drunkards fall out and break each other's heads, the unmerited aspect of the suffering is subject in the minds of most people to some mitigation. When very small girls are raped by full-grown men there is no possibility that public opinion will do other than condemn their actions. The suffering imposed is seen as totally unmerited and the attack totally unjustifiable. Offences committed by men in the 'random' victim category varied from the slightly ludicrous to the horrific.

The 'phantom cyclist', for example, leaped from his bicycle, groped at the bosoms of solitary and presumably startled women pedestrians and then pedalled off furiously, his strange but modest passion fulfilled. Another man, less modest in his appetites, held prisoner at his house a girl aged four and during the single night of her captivity raped her four times.

In the more violent cases, which are few, there is some emphasis on enforced fellatio which contrasts markedly with the normality of the sexual content in other encounters. Touching with the hands, the apposition of the organs, straight old fashioned intercourse or attempts at it, and a handful of would-be buggeries define the repertory of most of these sex offenders. Oral contacts and postural variants do not figure in most of the accounts provided in the police reports to prison governors. That may be a reflection of a mainly working-class sample of people, and a reported tradition of simplicity and directness in sexual matters which looks on middle-class practices of foreplay and postural variety as effete or deviant. Alternatively a simple lack of practice in conditions favouring experiment or novelty might account for the fumbling and ineffective nature of most of the behaviour which brought the sexual Forty Threes to court in the first place.

Two or three of the heterosexual offenders in this group live up to the labels which are pinned on them by other prisoners during their recruitment to Rule Forty Three. Most fall short of the widely quoted stories about the man who uses razor blades to gain access to the bodies of little girls. Whether he exists or not, this offender never made an appearance amongst the men at Shepton Mallet. The range of seriousness and the variety of the situations described here confirm that the selection of men for Rule Forty Three does not proceed along purely rational lines and that, as in racial prejudice, one characteristic is singled out to represent all the other ascribed demerits; for black skin read recorded sex offence.

Homosexual Offenders

The twenty-seven men convicted of homosexual offences against boys possess, naturally enough, a quite different profile. They are, to begin with, disproportionately numerous. In 1968, 1,940 men appeared before magistrates in England and Wales charged with sexual offences against females, but only 1,275 were dealt with for sexual offences against males, i.e.: a 3:2 ratio.[4] In 1968 the higher courts imposed prison sentences of more than one year on 169 offenders against males and on 448 offenders against females. Since both types of offenders appear to receive equivalent lengths of sentence, it is a reasonable assumption that the total sex offender population in prison at any one time should reflect those proportions.

Table 3.2
Sex offenders in magistrates courts; sent to prison by
higher courts; and in Shepton Mallet prison.

Type of offence	Convicted in magistrates courts, 1968		Sent to prison for more than 12 months by higher courts, 1968		Sample 100, Shepton Mallet, 1968	
	No.	%	No.	%	No.	%
Against Males	1,275	39.6	169	27.4	27	45.7
Against Females	1,940	60.4	448	72.6	32	54.3

In the Shepton population, however, offenders against males and against females are fairly evenly represented. There would therefore appear to be some degree of bias in the Rule Forty Three selection process towards the recruitment of offenders against boys. With heterosexual offences the object is of the right sex but the wrong age; with homosexual offenders both object and age group are wrong. But the virtual absence from the Shepton mens' victims of boys or girls aged over sixteen is not necessarily significant. More than four-fifths of all sex offence victims are under the age of sixteen according to the Cambridge Report on Sexual Offences.[5]

Homosexual offences frequently form part of a pattern of generalised sex activity with boys, sometimes culminating in attempts at buggery, but rarely, in these cases at any rate, achieving it. In only five instances were men in this group actually charged with a successful (from the offender's point of view) act of buggery. To some extent this may be due to the difficulty of obtaining evidence from reticent victims. Violence was used in one case, an attempted murder which followed an indecent assault on a boy of eight. Even more than with the girl victims one can often assume a consenting, collaborative and even a continuing sexual relationship between offender and offended. Two kinds of boy victims can in fact be distinguished; the 'collaborative' and the 'random'. The collaborative victims attracted two kinds of offender, 'The Cottagers' and 'The Conspirators'.

'Cottagers'

A homosexual 'cottage subculture' can be glimpsed in some of the offence details; men hanging round public lavatories in parks and other secluded places or frequenting fair grounds and amusement arcades.[6] They get to know boys who go there, some of whom are 'wise' too. Sexual activities often continue over a period of time and prosecution ensues when the behaviour is inadvertently brought to light. The scene for these activities is frequently a park or some other isolated spot, or it can be in the house, flat or room of the offender.

CASE SEVEN. A forty-four-year-old single man living with his elderly mother. After a grammar school education he had held a series of poorly paid jobs in service occupations: catering, warehousing, etc. The police report says that "He spends most of his leisure time hanging round public toilets, visiting cinemas and parks where young boys are normally to be found." The preferred form of his activities is expressed in a police description of two of this offences. "He indecently exposed himself to one boy and later indecently assaulted another boy placing his hands on the boy's private parts."

Three years for incitement to gross indecency.

CASE EIGHT. A twenty-eight-year-old ex-soldier working as a hairdresser and moving frequently from one place to another, took a job in a seaside town. At a fairground he met a group of twelve- to fourteen-year-old boys and took two of them back to his flat. Over the next six days the three of them engaged in mutual masturbation, fellatio and 'attempted' buggery.

Twelve months for indecent assault and attempted buggery.

'Conspirators'

'Conspirators', on the other hand, pursue involved strategies to gain the trust of parents as well as children so that they can take them off either for part of the day or for holidays. The pay-off in these cases is very long term and the risks of detection high, but one man was able to run his own children's club for almost three years, buggering meanwhile some of its young and uncomplaining members until a casual remark gave him away.

CASE NINE. A former youth worker aged thirty-five, ex-navy regular, with previous convictions for sexual offences against boys, befriended a family and gained the confidence of the parents to an extent where they were prepared to allow their sons to go with him for a holiday in a rented cottage in Cornwall. Whilst there he contrived to share a bed with each of the boys in turn and then "handled their private parts". No violence was used, no escalation of the activities took place and they continued intermittently for six months after the holiday before

they were accidentally discovered and he was prosecuted.
Three years for indecent assault.

As with heterosexual offenders it is also possible to distinguish two further categories amongst the homosexuals; the 'respectable' and the 'disorganised'. The 'conspirators' tend to be 'respectable' and to engage in 'good works' in the community.[7] But church-going and youth work can mean more to these men than mere disguises for their deviance; they are sometimes the means of achieving it. Other 'respectable' men are married, hold down reasonable jobs and are generally conformist in matters other than their sexual interests.

The 'disorganised' in the homosexual group differ from the heterosexual offenders by not being married. Instead of committing their offences within a fractured family setting, they seem to lead rather anomic lives: homeless, jobless, aimless, wandering about the country and allowing occasional expression to their sexual urges.

Finally there are the 'hand-holders'; men who approach quite young boys in the street and lead them by the hand to a more private place where the sexual activity takes place.

CASE TEN. A thirty-three-year-old ex-approved school boy, with no family, no fixed address, no job and a growing record of sexual assaults "approached a seven-year-old boy in the street. He took hold of the boy's hand and walked along the street. He took the boy into a derelict house and into an upstairs room. He then told the boy to lie on the floor, which the boy did, and then he took the boy's trousers off. He then took out his penis and tried to insert it into the boy's anus, lying on top of him in the attempt."
Four years for attempted buggery.

There were no cases in the sample of homosexual offences against a man's own children, and only two instances where a related child was concerned.

At the Seaside

A somewhat unexpected discovery was that fourteen of the

twenty-seven homosexual offenders lived in seaside towns or inland spas, not major ports like Liverpool or Portsmouth, but small holiday resorts and watering places, more particularly those in the south of England. Eleven of the thirty-two heterosexual offenders also came from seaside addresses, but only six of the thirty property offenders did so, four of those being from ports rather than resorts. Intriguing questions are posed by this finding as well as possibilities for future research.

Table 3.3 Rule Forty Three men living at the seaside

Address	Offence			Total
	Sexual			
	male victim	female victim	Property	
Seaside	14	11	6	31
Elsewhere	13	21	24	58
Total	27	32	30	89*

$X^2 = 6.30$ df 2 p $< .05$
*Excludes 11 violence cases.

For the pedophile homosexual the seaside is a happy hunting ground. It offers a great many locations where casual contacts with the target age group can be contrived: the beach, open spaces, a plethora of public lavatories, amusement arcades, cafes and snack bars, fairgrounds, piers and pleasure parks, cinemas, bowling alleys, swimming pools. Also on offer in season is a population of holiday makers whose everyday beliefs are, as it were, suspended. People on holiday entertain pleasurable expectations of opportunities to act out of role; to sport a leisure uniform; to take decisions governed by only a short-run hedonism and the available supply of spending money. Permission is given and taken to speak to strangers and to allow expression to relationships which flourish like hothouse plants in the unreal and condensed experience of the holiday. The 'holiday romance' is the jewel in this libertine setting. It has many advantages. It is limited in time by the extent of the holiday; a week or two weeks. The passing nature of the participants, here today and gone tomorrow, frees them to some extent from the feelings of shame or regret they might experience in a continuing face-to-face situation.

The choice of partners is less constrained by considerations of social class. Clothing cues, occupational rankings, stratified leisure settings and residentially based identities are all absent or compressed into a narrow range. Opportunities of this sort must be perceived and seized on by the more permanent of the seaside residents as well as by the mobile army of seasonal workers which mans the boat stations, the bars, the counters and the kitchens of the whole holiday business.

The Non-Sex Offenders

It might be thought that a detailed examination of the non-sex offenders in the Rule Forty Three population would yield a portrait of the 'grass' in the English prison system. Recruitment stories showed, however, that the group is a far from homogeneous one. In certain respects its members resemble the two sex offence groups. Their criminal sophistication, for instance, spans driving without a tax disc and a half million pound fraud. Simple larcenies or breaking into property, mainly private houses, and stealing things from them account for a majority of their offences. Altogether the thirty-five men in the non-sex offender group were charged at their last court appearances with a total of seventy-one offences as shown in Table 3.4.

Table 3.4 Non-sex offences

			Offence			
	Entering property and stealing	Fraud	Simple larceny	Violence	Driving	Receiving	Total
Number of charges	27	16	13	9	4	2	71

In the official prison records, property offences merit even
less description than sexual ones and it is not possible to say
much about the context in which most of them took place. The
presence or otherwise of accomplices, the sizes of the hauls,
connections with organised routes for disposing of stolen goods,
membership of gangs or underworld affiliations; virtually none
of this is to be obtained from the prison files, although occasional remarks in police reports do sometimes indicate a degree
of criminal involvement.

Twenty-four of the men had been sentenced on multiple
charges and a straight comparison cannot be made with the total
prison population classified by nature of offence; but there are
more convictions for fraud, false pretences and forgery than
would be the case in a perfect cross-section of the ordinary
prison population. That may be related to 'informing'; for the
stereotype of the fraud man is of someone possessing a
chameleon like quality which allows him to adapt socially to
whatever circumstances he encounters; now laughing with the
boys, now 'grassing' them to the 'screws'. Being all things to all
men is the stock-in-trade of the cheat and the false pretender,
but when discovery threatens or actually happens he can usually
count on his mobility and adaptability to evade the consequences. In prison he can run no further than the wing office,
and protection status is his only real sanctuary from the wrath
of betrayed fellows.

Beyond this simple classification of the non-sex offenders in
terms of their offences it is difficult to identify groupings of
the kind which could be seen quite clearly amongst the sex
offenders. It is proposed, therefore, to treat them as a single
group for the purpose of comparing them with the two sex
offender groups, the male and the female. And in comparing
them it may be possible to isolate some pointers to the nature
of the group life thought likely to emerge from the concentration of these men in the protection wing at H.M. Prison,
Shepton Mallet.

Two types of retrospective data about each man had been
collected; one set of items dealing with personal characteristics

such as age, address, marital status, occupation, religion; and another set having to do with criminal histories, such as number and type of previous convictions, length of current sentence, experience of institutions including approved schools, borstals, mental hospitals and prisons, and the amount of time spent in them prior to current sentence.

Personal Details

The men at Shepton, divided into their offence categories, were aged as follows:

Table 3.5 Age by offence

				Age				
Offence	21—24	25—29	30—34	35—39	40—44	45—49	50+	Total
Male	2	6	6	1	6	2	4	27
Female	0	5	4	10	5	5	3	32
Family violence	0	3	2	0	1	0	0	6
Property	5	9	4	3	5	4	0	30
Violence	1	1	2	0	0	0	1	5
Total	8	24	18	14	17	11	8	100

More of the 'female' men are aged over thirty-five compared with both the 'male' offenders and the property cases. By themselves, though, the ages of these men are not all that informative, since it is the nature of their longer experience of the world both outside and inside prison, which is more likely to determine the part they play or do not play in the inmate society. A stronger, though still crude, index of attachment to conventional values in the outside world may be sought in the married statuses of the men.

More than half the heterosexual offenders were married, as might have been expected, but the unmarried states of the property offenders and the homosexuals were of somewhat

Table 3.6 Marital status by offence

Status

Offence	Married	Separated/ Divorced	Single	Total
Male	3	4	20	27
Female	19	5	8	32
Family violence	5	1	0	6
Property	4	11	15	30
Violence	0	0	5	5
Total	31	21	48	100

different complexions. A third of the thieves had been married at some time and then separated or divorced, whereas more than two-thirds of the homosexuals had never been married at all. And, since the table was based on the information recorded at the time of latest conviction, it does not accurately reflect the mid-sentence position of those men described as 'married'. Nineteen of them had committed offences of either a sexual or a violent nature against their own children. And for thirteen of them the offences and the court proceedings which followed had apparently sounded the death knell for their marital relationships, which they were not intending to resume after completing their sentences. The six 'family' offenders who were due to return to their families after release comprised two 'respectables', two 'disorganised', and two 'disturbed' men. Seven of the twelve remaining married men had preserved their marriages apparently intact, and all of *them* had committed sexual offences outside of their families, which suggests the greater destructiveness of father—daughter offences.

Occupations

The quality of information in the official prison records is extremely variable, and in the case of the previous occupations of prisoners needs to be viewed with some scepticism. Even

police histories, which are often thoroughly researched documents, have not always been authenticated, and in many cases
the information on the file is provided by the man himself during
the reception procedures and not subsequently checked. So the
men at Shepton whose files proclaimed them to be an artist, an
actor, and a horse breeder based in Surbiton may have pursued
much more prosaic callings in reality; or even none at all. The
occupations for the one hundred men which were actually
recorded on the Initial Index Cards fell into three broad categories:

1. *Service* — which includes things like driving, catering and
   hospital work.
2. *Skilled* — mechanics, machinists, painters, masons, fitters,
   etc.
3. *Labouring* — mostly in the building trade.

There were also six men who had professional or clerical occupations, and five who were described as retired at the time of
their convictions.

Table 3.7 Occupation by offence

	Occupation					
Offence	Professional/clerical	Service	Skilled	Labouring	Retired	Total
Male	2	12	7	5	1	27
Female	2	7	11	11	1	32
Family violence	0	2	1	3	0	6
Property	2	4	10	12	2	30
Violence	0	0	0	4	1	5
Total	6	25	29	35	5	100

On the evidence of this table there were few differences
between the 'female' and property group in terms of occupations,
but there is a marked clustering of 'male' offenders in the
'service' column; a difference largely accounted for by a group
of drivers and seamen amongst the homosexuals.[8]

Religion

One lingering reminder of the role played by religion in the history of prison is the care with which recently sentenced prisoners are quizzed about their religious affiliations. Since for many prisoners these are purely nominal it may seem pointless to consider them at this point; but religion, as we shall see, plays an important part in the life of the Rule Forty Three wing.

Table 3.8 Religious affiliation by offence

Offence	Church of England	Roman Catholic	Non-conformist	Nil	Total
Male	14	3	5	4	26
Female	20	4	4	4	32
Family violence	6	0	0	0	6
Property	10	5	7	6	28
Violence	2	0	1	1	4
Total	52	12	17	15	96*

*Information missing on three men. One violence case — Jewish.

If the categories in this table are collapsed they yield statistically significant differences between the offender groups. 'Female' sex offenders are more likely than either the 'homosexuals' or the property offenders to be registered as Church of England. This may be a manifestation of what Laud Humphries has called the 'breastplate of righteousness', an outward display of religiosity and conformity which seemed to characterise men who took part in the casual homosexual encounters he studied in public lavatories in an American town.[9]

Criminal History

One of the constraints which acts against the formation of strong bonds in most inmate societies is the temporary and changing nature of their membership. The speed at which this changes is largely determined by the lengths of sentences being served by the individual prisoners who comprise a specific prison population at any particular time. At Shepton Mallet, the men in 'A' Wing were serving sentences of the following lengths:

Table 3.9 Length of sentence by offence

| | Length of sentence in years | | | | | | | | | | | |
Offence	1	2	3	4	5	6	7	8	9	10	More than 10	Total
Male	3	8	2	9	0	0	—	—	—	2	3	27
Female	2	3	6	3	5	5	—	—	—	5	3	32
Family violence	0	1	1	2	0	0	—	—	—	2	0	6
Property	3	4	5	6	3	4	—	—	—	4	1	30
Violence	0	0	2	2	0	1	—	—	—	0	0	5
Total	8	16	16	22	8	10	—	—	—	13	7	100

There is a curious gap in the lengths of sentences between six years and ten years, for which there is no obvious explanation, but which may be a distant echo of the days when penal servitude could only be dispensed in multiples of five years.

Compared to all prisoners in English prisons at the same time, the Shepton men were serving significantly longer sentences; more than twice as many of them had been sent to prison for three years or more than was the case nationally (76% compared to 35%). They were not, on that account alone, greatly different from the populations assembled in long-term prisons elsewhere in the prison system; and one of the reasons for the relative absence of shorter-term men would be the reluctance of governors to place such men on permanent Rule Forty Three by sending them to Shepton Mallet, for which there was, in any case, a waiting list.

As between the groups of offenders who made up the Shepton population, the homosexual offenders were serving shorter sentences than those of their heterosexual counterparts.

Previous Record

Length of sentence is not, however, simply a function of criminality as measured by previous convictions, since amongst the men at Shepton, those who were serving the *shortest* sentences, namely the property offenders, were also those with the *longest* records.

Table 3.10 Previous convictions by offence

Offence	Number of previous convictions						
	0	1—4	5—9	10—14	15—19	20+	Total
Male	3	11	2	4	6	1	27
Female	7	8	10	4	3	0	32
Family violence	1	2	1	2	0	0	6
Property	0	2	4	9	6	9	30
Violence	0	0	1	2	0	2	5
Total	11	23	18	21	15	12	100

It is indicative perhaps that neither the property nor the violence group possessed a single member for whom the current offence was the first ever, whereas for almost a quarter of the female offenders it was (significance p.<02). Such a difference has clear implications for the criminal identification or otherwise of the two groups, and also for the amount of time that members of the two major groups at Shepton had previously spent in prisons and other institutions.

Virtually all of the property offenders have been to prison before, so more of them have been exposed to inmate subcultures than is true of the sex offender groups, although a quite large proportion of them too have previous experience of life in a penal establishment of one sort or another. A small but interesting difference between the two types of sexual offenders is that the homosexuals are much more likely than the heterosexual ones to have been in an approved school.

Table 3.11 Previous institutional experience by offence

Offence	None	Approved school	Borstal	Prison	Total in group
Male	7	7	3	19	27
Female	10	1	3	17	32
Family violence	2	1	3	2	6
Property	1	4	11	27	30
Violence	0	1	1	5	5
Total	20	14	21	70	100

Institutions

Finally, not only have more of the property offenders been to prison than either 'male' or 'female' offenders, but they have spent more time there as well.

Table 3.12 Total prior time spent in prison by offence

Offence	Average number of months in prison
Male	42
Female	32
Property	65

On all these counts it is clear that there are fundamental differences between the three major groupings which have been identified in the Shepton population; differences in biographical detail and criminal history; differences which have a direct bearing on the possibilities of co-operation between the Rule Forty Three men and on the style of the interaction which was likely to emerge in any community they were able to construct for themselves on the protection wing.

Notes

1. Police departments were extremely efficient in sending reports on these offences, but their format and content varied widely from one force to another. Actual offence behaviour is a matter of great concern to the police and, in the case of a not guilty plea, to the court as well. But once a conviction is secured the precise details of the activity cease to be of such significance to the legal-penal system. Probation reports often omit any detailed discussion of the offence, and sentences often seem to reflect previous convictions more than current behaviour.

2. See Julia S. Brown, A comparative study of deviations from sexual mores, *American Sociological Review*, 17, 1952.

3. See below in Chapter 6, Salvation, Sponsorship and the Case of Adjacent Witches, for a discussion of the religious beliefs professed by Rule Forty Three men.

4. *Criminal Statistics*. England and Wales. 1968, HMSO. Cmnd. 4098.

5. *Sexual Offences*, A Report of the Cambridge Department of Criminal Science, Macmillan, London, 1957.

6. There is no English study to confirm the presence here of subcultures like those described by Laud Humphreys in *Tea-room Trade*, Aldine, Chicago, 1970, but quite clearly certain public lavatories do serve as meeting places for some homosexuals. The continuing activities of vice squad detectives in such places, some of them sporting tight white trousers suggests there is enough business there to support prosecutions for soliciting.

7. Laud Humphries, *op. cit.*

8. See also J. H. Fitch, Men convicted of sexual offences against children, A descriptive follow up study, *British Journal of Criminology*, Vol. 3, No. 1, July 1962.

9. Laud Humphries, *op. cit.*

CHAPTER 4

The Shape of the Community

Plural Ignorance

When asked about the extent and the nature of their relations with other Rule Forty Three prisoners, the men at Shepton Mallet were emphatic. "I keep to myself in here. I don't have anything to do with anybody. That only brings you trouble. I wouldn't trust anybody at all" was a typical comment by a long-serving thief. And the words of another man, "I never talk about myself. That's what it says in the rule book, never tell anybody anything about yourself. Keep to yourself." Come close to the classic prison prescription: 'Do your own time.'

Similar sentiments might be heard from almost any group of prisoners. They spring from a natural suspicion of equals who have all been recruited for some kind of villainy but they are also fostered by an official policy of divide and rule. Amongst the Forty Threes the pressures to voluntary isolation have been further reinforced by violent rejection at the hands of their peers and by subsequent, often prolonged, periods of solitary confinement. They have painful reasons for knowing that the sharing of knowledge about themselves can have undesirable consequences. Expressions of concern were even voiced about officers having access to the files in the wing office which contained details of offences.

Ideally, it seems, the individuals on protection sought to live together in pluralistic ignorance of each other's misdeeds. "I don't know what anybody else is in for. I don't want to know. I don't think anybody knows what I'm in for." The same words recurred in many accounts and they were linked to a passionate demand for equality amongst prisoners. "To my mind no prisoner has the right to judge another prisoner. I don't think anybody but God has the right to judge me. Cons don't have the right, because they're no better than me and I'm no better than them. We're all the same." And the reason: "We've all got to do our bird." 'Bird', the doing of time, is the great leveller before which all men in prison stand equal, in theory. But although the principle of plural ignorance is widely expressed and strongly held by the Rule Forty Threes at Shepton Mallet it is breached on countless occasions each day. Most of the violations occur in a constant flow of tale telling, tittle-tattle about what the other people in the wing are there for. So marked is the contrast between the unofficial rule of silence and the noisy reality of the wing that many of the individuals interviewed went out of their way to disclaim all interest in the gossip. "I don't listen to that kind of talk. I move away." "I hear people saying what other people are in for but I don't take any notice, some of the worst ones you hear about." "If any-one tries to tell me about someone I tell them to buzz off. There's one man here that's supposed to be in for going with an animal."

These quotations show that efforts to stem the flow of unwanted words were about as effective as a judge's order to a jury to ignore remarks already made in court. Once heard they will be remembered whether they are accurate or not. A lot of the 'common knowledge' held by the Forty Threes about each other was in fact as wide of the mark as that entertained by the non-Forty Three prisoners on 'C' wing. Thieves became buggers, buggers rapists, and rapists ran vans over their own children in the stories that circulated.

There are three aspects of these wholesale breaches in the most central value of the Forty Three community which merit further attention. Firstly the identification of sex and non-sex cases seems to be important, particularly for the thieves. Degraded as they already are by the 'grass' label, the thieves at Shepton are still anxious to distinguish themselves from 'sex pots'. A high status property offender, for example, said: "I sometimes talk to people in the yard and afterwards people say 'Do you know what he's in for?' I don't really want to know, but after that I can't walk round with him any more." There is also, in the interview material, a general feeling of fearfulness about homosexuals. "There's some really bent people here. I got put on a report the other day for refusing to take a shower. I was down there with about five other really bent blokes. I've seen 'em in there eyeing up the other blokes. Well you have a good laugh when its someone else, but not me." Or: "Homosexuals I just can't stand. They come up behind you and put their arms round you. I'd kick 'em to Kingdom Come if they touched me."

Fears of contamination from known 'queers' might appear not unreasonable for men deprived of their normal sexual outlets, but a few of the thieves were even more expressive about the heterosexual offenders. "If I ever got married again and had children outside and one of these sex pots came within a mile I'd run him over. I'd do life for it." This man's feelings about the pedophiles were expressed in a fierce solicitude for the safety of children as yet unborn. Another thief was equally vehement and illustrated a part of what may lie behind the more general prison attitude to sex offenders. "Of course they're not men in here. Only about twelve are men. The rest are sex cases. They just wouldn't walk in any other nick." And yet another property offender gave vent to feelings about sex cases that matched those of non-Forty Three men. "Well it's like imagining yourself doing things like that. You look at their faces and you think of them doing it. And you want to do them in. You can see it in their faces. I'm not saying I'm very handsome and they're all ugly, but you can tell. Sometimes I look at some of them and I think 'Christ, I can just imagine what you've done.' "

A second area of concern was with the identities of habitual grasses, possibly in self-defence, although practical fiddles were few at Shepton Mallet. A number of men were described as "always into the office" and presumably their company was avoided.

The third aspect of identification concerned what were considered to be the worst offences. The most gossipped about men were accorded very low status in the rudimentary hierarchy which was apparent in the wing. At the very bottom of the hierarchy of scapegoats were two men; one with a firm reputation as a 'grass', and another who had killed his own child. At different times they shared their uncrowded rung at the bottom of the Shepton community with two other sex offenders, one of whom was manifestly mad at the time. On the face of it none of the four seemed especially qualified for such an extreme position; neither on account of his offences nor for his current behaviour. These four men, at the time of this study, filled what appeared to be the lowest status positions within the lowest status group of the lowest status sector in English society. They represented the polar opposites in status terms of Her Majesty the Queen, in whose prison they found themselves confined by order of the courts.

Interaction

As to the quality of interaction which does take place between them, the Forty Threes report a hesitant and diffident style of getting along with each other. Its effect is to diminish any idea of personal involvement and to increase a sense of distance from other prisoners. "I speak when I'm spoken to and don't if I'm not" was a common phrase.

Holding aloof from fellow prisoners was rationalised in several ways. The high cost of personal involvement was sometimes referred to. Prison lore is full of stories about the broken promises of departed friends. The release of a mate is often an occasion to formulate all kinds of plans for action by proxy on behalf of the man left behind. Scores to be settled, errands run, personal messages delivered, effects collected, the welfare of wives or families to be attended to; a man may be released having memorised a long list of such undertakings. Fervent pledges are made during the euphoric 'gate fever' of the immediate pre-release period, but when the gates are banged shut behind him it is like a guillotine across a man's life. He is not officially allowed to write to his former friends and associates and the pressures of readjustment to the outside world soon crowd out or distort the commitments he has made. If the mate he left behind is soon to be released, he may keep to the arranged programme. If the period till the mate's release is longer, then advantage may be taken of the opportunities offered by access to personal belongings or to wives deprived of a husband's sexual presence. Sexual exploitation of wives or lovers during imprisonment is one of the things most likely to rob a man of the capacity to do his time. To a long sentence prisoner a divorce can even bring relief from the burden of forever worrying about a wife's fidelity. At Shepton Mallet such considerations affected only the few with continuing social ties, but the lack of relatives and friends outside actually increased the reliance placed on released friends to do favours of even a small kind.

Boredom and the limited returns from peer group partici-pation were also cited as reasons for voluntary isolationism. "I don't like it on association. There's not enough excitement to go round." And the personal characteristics of the other parti-cipants were thought to affect the benefits of contact. "They're so ignorant", 'childish' or 'depraved', men complained.

The opportunities for interaction were further constrained by a number of other factors. Of these, the work arrangements were probably the most important. At least a third of the Forty Threes were engaged in housekeeping and general administra-tion. Apart from the cleaners, who were numerous and worked together, these men were attached to officers and dispersed in ones or twos about the prison. Most of the remaining men were put to work reclaiming metal or mending 'Babycham' boxes in one of two shops in the outer yard. Given the staff role position from which this study was undertaken, it is not possible to report anything about what went on in the workshops.

Contacts between prisoners were also determined to some extent by the administrative and physical arrangements for evening 'association'. The privilege of 'association' was granted progressively to men as their sentences proceeded. The Forty

Threes who qualified were randomly allocated to two equally sized groups who took' 'association' out of their cells on alternate nights of the week. During these periods, a television set stood at one end of the wing, and the meal tables were available for playing cards or other games, or for just sitting and talking or reading. A dart board and table tennis table were set up at the recess end. On a typical night the men on association would be distributed equally between the television audience and the tables and games. Little movement took place, except to the recesses, or to the hairdresser or onto and off the tennis table. Seating in front of the television set was a highly patterned arrangement and friends or mates would sit together. But consistently adjacent positions did not necessarily imply friendship: "I go down on association three nights a week but I don't talk to anyone. I usually watch the TV and sit next to Ron Peel. Not because I particularly like Ron Peel; not because I particularly dislike him. Or anybody else."

In summary, the preferred style of interaction between Forty Threes as depicted in these interviews is that of a cool dissociation of equals. These inmate values subscribe to what may be called a 'cool' culture. The 'cool' culture is one that approaches in principle and precept the 'official' view of prison life and of all that is conducive to the establishment and maintenance of the 'quiet nick'. The 'quiet' nick and the 'cool' culture represent in fact the official and the informal aspects respectively of the same thing; the achievement of a stable order within the prison. 'Official' is not here synonymous with 'straight' culture since the behaviour expected of the ideal prisoner in the institution is not at all what conformity in the outside world demands. Outside, the 'straight' culture rests on the operation of largely internalised constraints on behaviour which are implicit in given social situations. In prison the constraints are highly and heavily explicit in the shape of the walls and the warders and the rules that govern the daily routine. 'Straight' culture outside demands self-controlled participation and competition in economic activities both as producers and as consumers. It also demands the exercise of responsibility for the ordering of personal sex relations. None of these is necessary under the 'official' prison code which reduces the complex, interlocking roles and multiple decisions of outside life to one simple injunction "Do your own time."

A conjunction of the 'official' ideology and a 'cool' culture brings obvious benefits to the staff in terms of control and quietude, but what is there in it for the inmates? To attempt an answer to that question is to enter the whole debate about the origins and functions of the inmate subculture and its contribution to the achievement of equilibrium within an institution. An answer to it may be clearer if institutional equilibrium is seen as a product of interacting 'cool' and 'hot' elements in the prison situation. Prisons are full of potentially 'hot' items; the compression of unruly participants into rigid and restrictive regimes; separation from sexual opportunities and families; the known dishonesty of most, and the violence of some prisoners; the struggle for status; limited availability of supplies, power and possessions. 'Cool' elements are less salient; staff pressures and inducements; and inmate social types who are predisposed to passive conformity are all ordinarily present. Rule Forty Three prisoners contain a high proportion of the latter type of prisoner and their previous violent experiences have added a further 'cool' dimension to the situation. The functional nature of privacy and the concealment of personal data is the most important 'cool' item at Shepton and it is underlined by the interview material on which this account has been based. But whatever they said in interviews about their resistance to gossip and their preference for their own company, most of the men on the protection wing spent their 'free' time, during evening and weekend association and the daily periods of exercise, either talking to, or walking with other prisoners.

On the Yard

Twice a day, for at least half an hour and sometimes longer, the prison day in England and Wales is punctuated by a ritualised activity called 'exercise'. In the days of the silence rule it

entailed endless, single file processions around a series of con-
centric circles, laid out like a target on the yard.[1] The eventual
removal of this rule allowed prisoners to make free and recurring
mutual choices of companions. These daily choices can be easily
observed and recorded in a form which constitutes a neat socio-
metry of the group of prisoners concerned.

During one calendar month (March 1968) twenty-eight daily
recordings were made of exercise periods in the small yard at
Shepton. Mostly these were the weekday morning periods but
on four days recordings were made both morning and afternoon.
The observations were made from a third floor window over-
looking the yard. Typically, men emerged onto the yard in pairs
or trios which remained stable in membership throughout each
period of 'exercise'. Some degree of movement took place to
begin with, as friends arrived, and at weekends the scene was
more animated than usual. Whenever changes of membership
took place, the longest lasting of the groups were noted.

Of the eighty men at that time located in 'A' wing, fifty-
seven appeared more than once on the yard during the period
of observation. Their appearances and the contacts they made
were arranged as individual lists, giving in rank order of fre-
quency the men they had chosen as companions for their daily
rounds. Preliminary inspection of these lists showed that they
fell consistently into three segments.

1. One, two or three men, with whom exercise was shared on
   a large number of occasions;
2. A somewhat larger group representing choices on an intermediate number of occasions; and
3. An even larger group of men with each of whom exercise
   had been taken on one or two occasions only.

Using the top three names from each man's yard record a
list of overlapping first order choices was constructed. Starting
with a property offender and working through all fifty-seven
men, the process was rather like that of developing a photograph. The outline of what appeared to be the social structure
of the protection wing at Shepton Mallet emerged with some
clarity. It contained twelve groupings of men. They ranged in

size from self-contained pairs and triads to groups containing four, five and six members and two larger ones with nine and twelve members respectively. These groups are listed in Table 4.1 with members' offence types.

The most salient fact about the groups is that A, B and C possess almost purely non-sexual memberships. The pairs and trios tended to be either homo- or heterosexual in character. Groups D and E were of mixed offender compositions; and group F was made up of four offenders against children; two violent, two sexual. The nine members of group G on the other hand, were with one exception, 'female' sexual offenders.

Considerable thought had been given to the possible bases of association which might be found amongst the Forty Threes. Potentially many, they would not necessarily be visible to the naked eye. Apart from nature of offence, friendships and

Table 4.1 Groups on the exercise yard

| | Offence | | | | |
| | | | Sex | | |
Group	Property	Violence	'Male'	'Female'	Total
A	4	0	0	(1)*	5
B	2	2	0	0	4
C	3	2	0	0	5
D	8	0	3	1	12
E	2	1	2	1	6
F	0	2	1	1	4
G	0	0	1	8	9
H	0	1	2	0	3
I	0	0	0	3	3
J	0	0	2	0	2
K	0	0	2	0	2
L	0	0	0	2	2
Total	19	8	13	17	57

* Adult rapist.

coalitions were thought possible along a number of dimensions: age, marital status, length of sentence, prior record, attitudes, occupation, physical location on the landings, etc. In the event, besides the basic sex/non-sex division one factor stood out quite plainly as binding together the members of certain groups; and that was regional origin. The first group of five, A, consisted of two Irishmen, two Scotsmen and an Englishman. The second group of four, B, had as principal members two Welshmen with two Englishmen in attendance. The third group, C, was made up exclusively of Yorkshiremen and all but two of the twelve members of the fourth, D, were drawn from a region which can be identified as Wessex.[2]

Table 4.2 Regional origins of yard group members

Group	Number of men	Regional origins
A	5	Celtic
B	4	Welsh/English
C	5	Yorks
D	12	Wessex

The Wessex group was in fact made up of two sub-groups held together by one man; a first time 'family' sex offender. Linked to him on one side are three other sex offenders who do not themselves have many links with the non-sex members of the Wessex group. There are therefore two groups, D and E which straddle the sex/non-sex line that cuts across the social structure of the prison community at Shepton Mallet. This structure, together with an indication of the linkages between groups, is set out in Fig. 4.1. The Celts and the four members of group F are at opposite ends of the inmate system and no direct links exist between them. Group E occupies a clearly pivotal position, being connected with many of the sex offender groups as well as non-sex Wessex men.

The other groups — Wessex, Welsh and Yorks — are intermediate, both in the social-spatial sense of the diagram and in

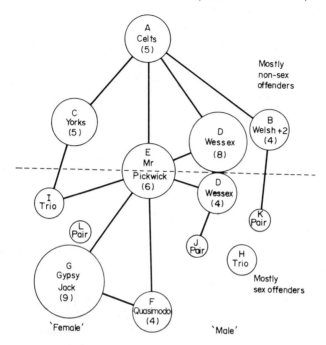

Fig. 4.1

terms of offender composition. Wessex, as we have seen, divides into a non-sex component and a sex one. Both the Welsh and the Yorks groups contain members (one and two respectively) convicted of violence against children, but two of the three also possess long criminal records and prior institutional sentences for property offences.

Unexpectedly, the homosexual groupings are virtually exclusive and have nothing to do with each other. They also have somewhat stronger secondary connections with the non-sex side of the line than with the 'female' dominated groups. These cross line ties are tenuous ones but may be related to some of the results presented in the last chapter. On a number of dimensions, such as age and length of sentence, the homosexuals fall between the female and the property men. In particular the age range of the homosexuals and the property men is quite close. The connection is not however explained by homosexual offenders having more non-sexual criminal offences to their credit than the 'females', since the reverse is in fact the case.

The Internal Structure of the Groups

Three classes of association are discernible in the sociometric data: cohesive primary groups; aggregates of semi primary groups, and isolated dyads and triads. Cohesive primary groups such as the Celts and the Welsh provide a relatively exclusive framework within which intensive contacts between members are recorded. The Wessex and some of the 'female' groups on the other hand consist of numbers of smaller groupings with overlapping memberships.

Status within each group can be inferred from the position of each member in the lists of association frequencies for all the other men in the group. Amongst the Celts there was a small red-haired Scot who, with his scars, his broken teeth and a hate stare of Southern State intensity, exuded an air of physical menace. He came top of the list for all four other members of the group. He clearly saw himself as a hard man and although, so far as I know, never actually molested anybody in the wing, was accorded great deference. His association pattern was one of almost unalloyed purity. Only six of his forty-eight recorded contacts were with non-Celts. Other Celts averaged ten contacts each outside the group. A rank ordering of mutual choices in this group revealed an inner triad comprising the boss Scot and two Irish cronies. The remaining two Celts were a rapist with a long property offence record as well, and a former tobacco baron from another prison who had given evidence in court which implicated not only the 'screw' who was bringing in the precious 'snout' but other inmate 'fiddlers' too.

Leadership was less clearly marked in the other group. The Welsh/English faction for instance was based on a strong dyad.

But in each of the remaining aggregates there were men who could be called leaders of sorts. Amongst the Wessex men they were:

1. A forty-four-year-old man with the longest prison record in the group, whose face, to quote another prisoner, was 'the personification of evil' but behind which lay a warm and prison wise personality. Immediately around him were gathered three men with convictions for fraud type offences.
2. A young Cornishman, twenty-eight, with an impressive total of convictions and institutional experiences behind him but no other apparent attributes to explain his popularity.
3. A first-time prisoner convicted of a family sex offence and who formed the link between the upper and lower Wessex groups.

Equally diffuse leader types appeared amongst the other groupings.

1. A large, benign looking, ungainly man in his mid-forties, rather like Mr Pickwick in appearance, convicted of offences against a young teenage girl which were described by a judge as 'lewd and despicable' had been in prison once before for similar offences. He refused all association during the evening but on the yard he led a mixed composition group including both homosexual and non-sexual offenders.
2. 'Gypsy Jack'; another middle aged man doing nine years for what amounted to rape. Although not himself a 'family' offender, he was the central figure in a loose group of nine men who mostly fell into that category. His attitude towards all prison staff was acid and resentful, but with his peers he gave off gaiety and good humour.
3. 'Quasimodo'; self-styled 'fat and ugly', held together a singular group of outcasts. Only six of the fifty-seven men who appeared on the yard during the observation period walked round by themselves on more than one occasion. Three of them fell into Quasimodo's orbit; Quasimodo

himself and two men who appeared to be classic paranoid schizophrenics. The other member of this group, who made few excursions onto the yard, was the man most often quoted by other prisoners when relating the awful deeds of their fellows. He was said to have thrown his infant son on the fire and held him there with his foot until he burned to death. What he had actually done was to beat the child's head against a wall, which was bad enough in any case, but not quite so horrific as the rumour. The two remaining solo walkers were an exceptionally embittered non-family sex-offender and a pedophile homosexual member of the Wessex group.

Finally, it can be seen from Table 4.1 that these groups account for fifty-seven men altogether. At the time the recordings were made, the total population of the Rule Forty Three wing was eighty. Who were the twenty-three men who never appeared on the yard? In theory obligatory exercise was in practice optional. The wide distribution of appearance totals between one and twenty-eight indicates the degree of informal control which it was possible for individuals to exercise over their outings. Negotiation with staff; illness real or claimed and governor's application, could be used to avoid exposure to the weather or to fellow prisoners. The absentees were not just the most skilled in this activity but were also the men who had been appointed to positions of trust by the staff. They performed clerical, cleaning and construction tasks on behalf of the administration; 'trusties' in other words. They constitute an additional but absent segment to the structure shown in Table 4.1.

In this chapter some evidence has been presented about what Rule Forty Three prisoners say, and appear to believe, about each other; and about the nature of their interaction. And we have seen, using the yard data, how they hang together in groups which together constitute the social structure of Shepton Mallet. Chapter 5 will look in more detail at some of the attitudes and activities of the group members.

Notes

1. The movement of the Rule Forty Three men in the yard at Shepton
    was always in an anti-clockwise direction. On a few occasions some
    non-Forty Three prisoners were put into the yard at the same time to
    take exercise. They all stuck together and walked round the inside of
    the moving circle but in the opposite direction to that taken by the
    Forty Threes.
2. 'Wessex' here means central, southern and south western England,
    with Bristol, Oxford and Portsmouth marking its northern and eastern
    most boundaries.

CHAPTER 5

Conformists and Critics

Conformists

Each new entrant to prison is faced with a dilemma. The official expectation of him is that he will be respectful and obedient and hard working, and that he will heed advice to 'do his own time'. Other prisoners, however, put pressure on him to become part of the inmate subculture; to reject the staff view of things and to support or take part in a variety of forbidden activities. Different prisoners solve this problem in different ways, but the overall pattern of their solutions dictates the nature of the atmosphere which prevails in a prison at any particular moment in time. The factors which influence this crucial choice are clearly of great interest to students of prison social organization.

Donald Clemmer's contribution to this field was to describe a process he called 'prisonisation'.[1] By this he meant the socialisation of individual prisoners to the anti-staff norms of the inmate culture. He appears to have seen this as a linear process; the longer a man spends in the company of other prisoners the more likely it is that he will come to share their view of prison officials. Some men would be immune to such pressures, and some would resist longer than others, but the general drift would be towards conformity with the values of the inmate subculture.

Two strands of inquiry have followed from Clemmer's work. One seeks to explain 'prisonisation' almost entirely as a response to the conditions of imprisonment itself; the other argues that men bring with them from the outside world personal qualities which lead them to adopt defined inmate roles within the prison. Don Gibbons has characterised these two positions as the 'structural' and the 'importation' theories, respectively.[2]

Wheeler has explored the first of these themes and demonstrated that 'prisonisation' is not necessarily a straightforward deepening of anti-staff attitudes over time.[3] He has shown that many men enter prison professing attitudes which are essentially pro-social in character. As their sentences proceed towards a midpoint these attitudes change in an anti-social direction. Then as the ends of their sentences approach, their views tend to revert to what they were on entry, thus describing, according to Wheeler, a 'U'-shaped curve of conformity. A similar curve has been confirmed by other students,[4] although dissenting conclusions have also been reported.[5] Looked at in isolation, these findings lend support to the view that anti-social sentiment amongst prisoners is mainly generated by the deprivations of life inside, by the 'pains of imprisonment', and that it is a functional adaption to them.

Clarence Schrag, on the other hand, has attempted to integrate some of the known pre-sentence characteristics and values of prisoners with their behaviour within the institution, in terms of the roles they play there.[6] He distinguishes four principal role types for prisoners: the 'square john', the 'politician', the 'right guy' and the 'outlaw', each of which, he says, displays a specific combination of attitudes to authority and behaviour in prison. The 'square john', a pro-social man in Schrag's typology, is a non-professional offender, often serving his first prison sentence, either for violence, or sometimes for sex. He maintains strong social ties and continues to support conventional norms to an extent which excludes him from membership of many prisoner groupings. The 'politician', or pseudo-social offender, who is typically convicted of fraud or false pretence type offences, is someone possessed of the ability to conform easily to whatever situation he finds himself in. The 'right guy', or anti-social type, is usually a recidivist and a professionally identified offender strongly connected with a criminal subculture outside prison. He takes little part in inmate

activities but enjoys high status, provides a model of proper
conduct for other men and can sometimes crystallise anti-staff
feelings. The prison behaviour of the 'outlaw', or a-social man,
betrays an irrational or disordered personality, given to random
acts of violence which threaten inmates as much as staff.

Roles are regularly occurring patterns of behaviour within
groups; 'prisonisation' is a process which operates at the level of
the individual; the idea of a prison subculture embraces both of
them, together with their related norms and values. Donald
Cressey and John Irwin have sought to extend this basic concept by proposing that prisoners have the opportunity of sub-
scribing to not just one, but to three alternative subcultures.[7]
These subcultures, which they designate the 'thief', the 'convict', and the 'straight', overlap Schrag's role categories but
are not identical with them.

The 'thief' culture, they suggest, is one that has its referents
in the wider criminal society beyond the prison walls. 'Thieves'
draw status from their connections with big gangs or spectacular
'jobs' on the outside, and tend to hold aloof from what goes on
in the inmate world. 'Convicts', on the other hand, belong to a
subculture which is firmly based within the institution. Deviant
opportunities and the status to be derived from them are con-
strued in relation to 'fiddles' inside the prison, to trafficking,
and soft work assignments. The horizon of their expectations is
bounded by the prison walls. The third culture suggested by
Cressey and Irwin is that of the 'straight' men who conform to
the demands of legitimate authority both in and out of prison.
They tend to be first-time prisoners convicted of violence or
sexual assault. The maintenance of anti-social norms by the
'thieves' and the 'convicts' should, in theory, lead to greater
interaction between them. 'Straights', however, are more
likely to obey the injunction to 'Do your own time', and to
avoid too much contact, even with each other.

We would expect to find amongst the Rule Forty Three
population at Shepton Mallet a mixture of 'thieves', 'convicts'
and 'straights', but we would not expect them to be evenly
distributed between the three major offence groups: property,

male victims and female victims. In theory, members of the 'thief' culture would be located amongst the property offenders; 'straights' would be concentrated in the sex offender groups, with a bias possibly to greater representation amongst the 'female' offenders; and 'convicts' might be found in both.

A Measure of Conformity

Stanton Wheeler has made some attempt to measure the strength of anti-staff feeling in American prisoners, using a simple attitude questionnaire.[8] In particular he has applied this measure to a population of 'dings', men who are similar in some ways to the Forty Threes at Shepton.

Four of the items from Wheeler's questionnaire, modified to fit English prison life and language, were administered to fifty Rule Forty Three men. They were drawn from the men on 'A' wing who were not entitled to association on the evening chosen for the application of the questions, and who were therefore 'banged up' in their cells. Three or four men refused to complete questionnaires, and two did not complete them properly. A comparison of this group of fifty with the one hundred men on whom the study is based revealed no significant difference on any of the available variables.

The questions were presented as follows:

Here are some stories of incidents in prison life. Under the first three, are four statements, STRONGLY APPROVE, APPROVE, DISAPPROVE, STRONGLY DISAPPROVE. For each story underline the statement which is nearest to the way you feel about what the prisoner has done. For story number 4 underline the statement you agree with.

1. A prisoner is put on a work party at a flat rate wage. Some of the other men on the party criticise him because he does more work than anybody else. He works as hard as he can.

STRONGLY   STRONGLY
APPROVE   APPROVE DISAPPROVE DISAPPROVE

2. Prisoners Bluett and Parks are good friends. Bluett has a £1 note which has been smuggled into the prison. He tells Parks that the staff are suspicious and asks him to hide the money for a few days. Parks takes the money and carefully hides it.

STRONGLY   STRONGLY
APPROVE   APPROVE DISAPPROVE DISAPPROVE

3. A prisoner without thinking commits a minor offence against prison discipline. An officer who sees him puts him on report for it. Later, three other prisoners are talking about it. Two of them criticise the officer. The third prisoner defends the officer and says he was only doing his duty.

STRONGLY   STRONGLY
APPROVE   APPROVE DISAPPROVE DISAPPROVE

4. Two prisoners are planning an escape. They threaten to beat up another prisoner unless he steals a chisel for them from a workshop. He is afraid of them and whilst trying to smuggle the chisel into the wing is caught by an officer. He is put on report and stands to lose remission. He can get off the charge if he blames the other two prisoners.

   Should he make a statement about the other two?

   Should be keep quiet and take the blame?

The four point response scales to the first three items were dichotomised into pro- and anti-staff categories and combined with the response to item 4 to construct a conformity score for each man. The results are shown in Table 5.1. in terms of pro-staff responses.

Table 5.1 Conformity by type of offence

Offence	Number of pro-staff responses					
	0	1	2	3	4	
Property/violence	4	3	4	4	2	17
Male	0	1	7	4	3	15
Female	0	0	3	7	5	15
Total	4	4	14	15	10	47*

*Excludes 3 cases of family violence.

Although these figures fail to reach statistical significance they do show a marked concentration of anti-staff sentiment amongst the 'property' offenders and of pro-staff sentiment amongst the 'female' sex offenders. Even more significantly, the three members of the Celt group who completed the questionnaire all scored 'nil' on conformity.

Changes Over Time

Other parts of Wheeler's work which indicate a 'U'-shaped socialisation curve over time could not be adequately checked against the experience of these Forty Threes since the crucial first few months of their sentences had invariably been spent at other prisons before transfer to Shepton Mallet. Subsequent research by Garabedian using Schrag's typology has demonstrated differential responses or conformity curves during the course of a sentence.[9] He found, for example, that 'square johns' or 'straight' men exhibited the classical 'U'-shaped curve away from and back towards a position of conformity. At a lower level the same was true for 'right guys', the leaders of the inmate subculture who typified the qualities of the 'good con'. 'Politicians', or con-men, as well as the 'outlaws', violent, unpredictable prisoners, both moved progressively further away from a conformist position during the course of their sentences. 'Dings', on the other hand, a rag bag assortment of subcultural rejects and scapegoats by Wheeler's classification, start from a position of low conformity at the beginning of sentence and move consistently towards a highly conformist position by the time of release.

The smallness of the Forty Three questionnaire group does not permit any elaborate analysis of the development of conformity and non-conformity during current sentence. Added to that there is the difficulty inherent in making assumptions about changes over time from cross-sectional data gathered on one occasion only. Panel studies would be necessary for firmer conclusions than these. There were, however, some indications of an association both between conformist responses and the length of time elapsed on present sentence, and also more strongly with the total amount of time spent in prison prior to the present conviction. Men who had spent more than sixty months in prison on previous sentences were more likely to have high conformity scores than men who had spent less time than that inside:

Table 5.2 Conformity by total prior time served in prison

Total prior time served	Conformity score			
	0—1	2	3—4	Total
Nil	0	6	8	14
–60 months	7	6	7	20
60+ months	1	5	10	16
Total	8	17	25	50

Men with no previous prison time to their credit are quite conformist. Those who have spent up to sixty months inside include a proportion of non-conformists, but the men with very long prison careers tend to return towards the pro-social position. Echoes of this curve show up in the data for each of the three offender groups, 'male', 'female' and property.

No great reliance can be placed on findings from so few cases, but since the curves for each group are all in the same direction, they could be said to support the idea that there is a conformity curve which operates not just within the currency of a single prison sentence but during the course of a longer prison career spanning several sentences.

This possibility can be illustrated and expanded by cons-tructing a 2 × 2 box which plots the origins of inmate sub-cultures, outside or inside the institution; against the orientation of these subcultures towards prison staffs, 'pro' or 'anti'. Cressey and Irwin's three cultures can be quite easily located; the 'thief' culture, for example, originates outside the prison and is determinedly anti-staff in character. The 'straight' culture also has its roots in the outside world but has a fundamentally pro-staff complexion. The 'convict' culture springs out of the conditions which prevail inside prison but which give rise to anti-staff attitudes. The fourth box in the schema is one which is defined as arising within the institution but remaining pro-staff in outlook.

Men who fall into this category might be described as belonging to an 'institutional' culture.

In this form it represents no more than a logical possibility which, together with Cressey and Irwin's three categories could be operationalised and tested for empirically amongst particular prison populations. In the absence of such data it is still possible to visualise likely developments in attitudes to authority through time, and these have been indicated by the arrows on the diagram (Fig. 5.1).

If 'thieves' stay long enough inside they are most likely to move first to the 'convict' position, abandoning their disdain for the things of the prison world, and adopting the same

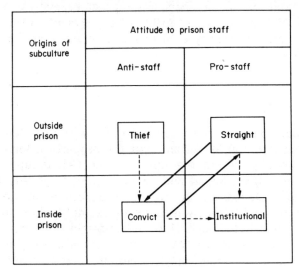

Fig. 5.1. Four prison subcultures.

opportunistic approach as their less principled peers. It is also possible that 'straight' men, rather than passing imperceptibly towards an 'institutional' perspective, may first be contaminated or colonised by long-serving 'convicts'. This would represent the classical process of prisonisation suggested by Clemmer. 'Wheeler's 'U'-shaped curve could also be super-imposed on the diagram to show the movement which takes place during a single sentence in the attitudes of certain men. The differential curves discovered by Garabedian would result in unilateral movements between the 'straight' and 'convict' boxes.

The evidence at Shepton Mallet suggested that all of these movements, either in one direction or the other or in 'U'-shaped curves might also hold good over the period of a criminal career involving several prison sentences. In those cases there is the additional possibility of movement into the 'institutional' position either directly from the 'straight' or indirectly from the 'thief' via the 'convict' cultures. It seems likely that the 'institutional', unlike the other three cultures, represents a terminal position and that its members, although superficially committed to pro-social values, are incapable of adjustment to the outside world where conformity demands a more active application of held values.

Critics

The data on conformity located the origins of potential dissidence at Shepton Mallet amongst the property offenders and most pointedly within the ranks of the Celt group. We saw earlier the self-contained and exclusive nature of this group's interaction. Opposition to the official regime, in word and thought, if not in deed, was therefore exemplified by one small group of men. High cohesion and anti-social sentiment were found to fit together for these few individuals. For the others; for the majority of the Forty Threes gathered together in conditions of free association, no similarly strong bonds of shared ideas or sentiments seemed to exist. If the closeness of an oppositional culture brings comfort to those who share it and sustains them in their struggle to retain reasonably satisfactory self-images; what equivalent or alternative mechanisms exist for those who tolerate or espouse, rather than actually despise, the position of the 'screws'?

Thomas Mathiesen has described what he calls 'censorious-ness' as one functional alternative to subcultural solidarity.[10] Besides the conventional deprivations of incarceration, the men at Ila, the Norwegian prison he studied were confronted by two additional threats to their self-conceptions. Firstly they faced the crippling uncertainty of indeterminate sentences, and secondly the systematic attempts of the prison regime to define them all as psychiatric cases; each to be treated according to his needs. Under such pressures, says Mathiesen, these men engaged in constant criticism of the staff and the regime, in ways designed to minimise the impact of 'individualisation', of discretion and thus of organisational uncertainty. Whether such criticism actually affected the behaviour of staff to any significant degree is difficult to gauge but, despite the wide-spread nature of the behaviour, it did not lead according to Mathiesen, to the development of solidary bonds, or the creation of any 'we' feeling in the ranks of the prisoners. It appeared to be a fundamentally individual strategy.

The burden of indeterminate sentences is not carried by most Rule Forty Three prisoners. In English law they are applied almost exclusively to men convicted of murder.[11] At the same time rejection by peers of the lowest social rank imaginable represents what might be seen as an equally serious assault on the identity. No previous test seems to have been made of Mathiesen's notions outside of his own study. Because of certain similarities between his population and that at Shepton Mallet, an attempt was made to measure 'censoriousness' and to relate it to other characteristics of the Rule Forty Three men. This was done initially by examining the formal com-plaints and requests for petition forms made by the men, and recorded in the 'A' wing office.

Formal complaints concerned a variety of issues, food, clothing, treatment by staff, and so on. Normally they were 'noted' and no further action was taken. Sometimes the Governor or the relevant member of staff would reject the complaint with varying degrees of indignation. Complaints by prisoners about staff have to be put with extreme delicacy since under the disciplinary code it is actually a punishable offence to make unjustified accusations against an officer. Petitions, of which more than fifteen thousand are thought to reach the Home Office each year, constitute a kind of harmless safety valve for the release of tensions generated within the institution.[12] Any man, at any reasonable time, may demand the appropriate form and writing materials with which to petition the Secretary of State about virtually anything. It is one in a series of expedients allowed to a man with a grievance about his trial or sentence or treatment in prison. First of all he can go on 'Governor's application' and state his point or case. If he does not receive satisfaction there he may then petition or ask to see a member of the Visiting Committee. When, and only when, he has exhausted those options a man may write to raise a point with his Member of Parliament. Eventually on particular points he may write to the European Court of Human Rights.

A few petitions to the Home Office lead to action. The majority, after what appear to the prisoner to be interminable and unnecessary delays, come back with a stereotyped note attached which begins "The Secretary of State has considered ... and sees no case for changing the decision. . . ." Petitions are used for all sorts of purposes. Immediately after sentence they are used in connection with appeals or to secure transfers to prisons more convenient for family visits. The purely legal uses of petitioning diminish as time passes and more personal ones take their place. Asking for a petition form is sometimes held by prisoners to be a mild sanction against unacceptable staff behaviour since whatever they may write on it, whether true or not, the officer who is named on it will be invited to comment in his own defence. Potentially, if not too often in practice, it is an embarrassment to individual staff members.

"It keeps them on their toes" as one well-practised complainer put it. Just over half of the one hundred men in this study had recorded no complaints or requests for petition forms during their stay at Shepton Mallet. Thirty had complained or asked for petitions on one or two occasions only, and the remaining eighteen had done so more frequently.

Table 5.3 Number of complaints and petitions

	Number of complaints and petitions			
	0	1—2	3+	Total
Number of men	52	30	18	100

Of the eighteen frequent complainers, seven had present or previous convictions for violence, mostly against adults rather than children. Six were convicted of buggery or attempted buggery; three for offences against girls, and two for larceny.

These totals cannot, however, be directly compared with other data and must first of all be related to the amount of time which each man had spent at Shepton Mallet. Altogether the one hundred men studied had spent 1,151 months at the prison between its opening in September 1966 and the end of the study period in June 1968, an average stay of 11.5 months per man. Fifty-five complaints and seventy-two petitions were recorded for these men in the 'A' wing office during that time. That works out at 0.09 complaints/petitions per man, per month.

An expected complaints and petitions score for each man was derived by multiplying the number of months he had spent at Shepton by 0.09. These expected scores were then subtracted from the actual complaints and petition totals for each individual. The results, representing a time-corrected complaints rate, ranged from +10.47 to −1.89. These were arbitrarily divided into three: high scores were defined as more than 0.5; medium, as between +0.5 and −0.5; and low as less than −0.5.

Table 5.4 sets out the complaints and petition scores for the fifty men who answered the conformity questionnaire, who were used for this part of the analysis so that the scores on both dimensions could be directly compared.

Table 5.4 Complaints and Petitions

	Low	Medium	High	Total
Number	14	26	10	50

It was not possible in fact to establish any significant relationships between complaints and conformity; but complaints and petition scores *were* significantly related to a number of other items. These can be grouped together to form two profiles; those of the 'high' and the 'low' complainers.

The 'high' complainers in the group of fifty had more previous convictions than their colleagues, and had been to prison more often. They were also more likely to have been in a mental hospital at some time in their lives. And they were more often unmarried or divorced. The 'low' complainers on the other hand were disproportionately drawn from the 'female' sex offenders. They were further into their present sentences than other men. They were also more likely (in response to another of Wheeler's items not reported in this study) to rate highly the extensiveness of their contacts with other prisoners at Shepton Mallet.

These are not very elaborated profiles, but the more socially isolated, recidivistic and mentally unstable nature of the 'high' complaints group is consistent with Mathiesen's findings at Ila. As is the profile of the 'low' complainers. We have already seen that the 'female' offenders at Shepton Mallet fall most readily into the 'straight' culture proposed by Cressey and Irwin. As a group they are less criminally experienced, more connected to the outside world by ties of marriage, more religiously orthodox, and more conformist in their attitudes than either the homosexual or the property offenders. They are, on all these grounds, an unlikely source of recruits for the role of institutional critic.

These findings, although they are not conclusive, do suggest that for at least some of the men at Shepton Mallet, 'censoriousness', or constant criticism of the regime, did represent one way of coming to terms with their situation. Some of the less formal ways in which these kinds of criticism were used by prisoners to influence the behaviour of prison officers will be examined in a later chapter.

But conformist sentiment and complaint behaviour do not between them exhaust the repertoire of responses which Rule Forty Three men made to their prison environment. Of these, by far the most important, was the role that religion played in the life of the protection wing.

Notes

1. Donald Clemmer, *The Prison Community*, Christopher Publishing House, Boston, 1940.
2. Don C. Gibbons, *Society, Crime and Criminal Careers*, Prentice Hall, Englewood Cliffs, N.J., 1968.
3. Stanton Wheeler, Socialisation in Correctional Communities, *American Sociological Review*, 26, 1961.
4. Peter G. Garabedian, Social Roles and Processes of Socialisation in the Prison Community, *Social Problems* 11, 1963—4 and
   Daniel Glaser, *The Effectiveness of a Prison and Parole System*, Bobbs-Merrill, Indianapolis, 1964.
5. R. C. Atchley and M. P. McCabe, Socialisation in Correctional Communities — A Replication, *American Sociological Review* 33, 1968.
6. Clarence Schrag, A Preliminary Criminal Typology, *Pacific Sociological Review* 4, Spring 1961. Also by Schrag, Some Foundations for a Theory of Corrections in D. R. Cressey (ed.) *The Prison*, Holt Rinehart & Winston, N.Y., 1961.
7. D. Cressey and J. Irwin, Thieves, Convicts and the Inmate Culture, *Social Problems* 10, 1962.
8. Stanton Wheeler, *op. cit.*
9. Peter G. Garabedian, *op. cit.*
10. Thomas Mathiesen, *The Defences of the Weak*, Tavistock, London, 1965.
11. Apart from treason and murder, life sentences are also possible for men convicted of incest, rape or buggery.
12. This is an estimate provided by the Prison Department. Accurate records of the numbers of petitions received do not appear to be kept.

CHAPTER 6

Salvation, Sponsorship and the Case of the Adjacent Witches

Salvation

Translated into English, the American prison truism that "All rapos are bible backs' would read 'All sex cases are religious maniacs.' So far as the Shepton Mallet population of sex offenders is concerned, the proposition is not literally true, although some of the men there knew of the stereotype and applied it to their fellow prisoners. "Most of the ones I've known in the prisons have been the same", said one. There is, as we have seen, some evidence that the sex offenders are more likely to be registered as Church of England than are property offenders. And that the heterosexuals amongst them are even more likely than homosexuals to be 'C of E', although membership of the Established Church is not normally thought to signify religious mania.

What is perhaps more interesting is that of the one hundred men in the study population, as many as thirteen whilst at Shepton Mallet, took a keen interest in religious activity of a fundamentalist Protestant nature, and that a further five were involved to varying degrees with exotic religious beliefs and practices. Two of the fundamentalists were registered as Seventh Day Adventists, three as Elim Pentecostals and one as Church of God. Of the remaining seven, five were nominally Church of England, one was Nonconformist and one was a Catholic. Of the thirteen, nine were convicted sex offenders; five heterosexuals and four homosexuals. But it would not be correct to treat these co-religionists as a homogeneous and united group.

They formed and dissolved pairs and trios and temporary coalitions with a speed and complexity that did credit to the factional nature of the sects to which they confessed allegiance. And when the two further groups are added, the 'devout Church of England' and the 'exotic', it becomes increasingly difficult to say what social functions their specific beliefs and activities were actually serving.

It was certainly not a practical means of achieving solidarity, although the intention may have been there to begin with; "We all stick together. I think it helps to make a sort of community for ourselves. We can help each other in little ways. For instance Albert was always shouting out about sex cases; at the television he was always going on about it and picking on people. We used to stick together and ignore it." That was one man's interpretation of his own extremist religious grouping, but none of its other members spontaneously mentioned this collective aspect of their beliefs. In most cases they simply emphasised the benefits to themselves as individuals. Considering the traditional isolation of the sex offender on protection, it is not too surprising that religious sentiments seem to have a basis which is more personal than social. What these men appeared to be after as individuals was forgiveness for their offences; something which they did not find in the more established faiths. "I pray to God for forgiveness", said a recent convert to fundamentalism. "I used to be 'C of E' but now I'm Elim Pentecostal. I changed to it last year. I find it much easier to follow. The Church of England, *it's not a fully lenient religion.* I mean if you've done a crime, it's always with you. But with the Pentecostals you feel ashamed and you tell somebody about it and then you can go on from there. You can put it behind you. It's more definite and it comes from the scriptures, but in 'C of E' its too vague. *With Elims you know where you stand.*"

The man who said this was arguably one of the Rule Forty Three cases with the greatest need of all for absolution. He was the man who had raped a girl just four years old four times in a single night. Other prisoners elsewhere had made manifest the strength of *their* feelings about that by breaking his skull for him; and society's displeasure was written into his ten-year sentence. Neither had scourged his conscience to his own satisfaction. Something more was needed; and not just confession followed by a verbal absolution. Catholicism could offer the mechanics of that. The extra ingredient which this man, and others like him, were able to find in Elim was an element of salvation through hard work. "You know what you have to do. It means a lot of hard work. You have to do a lot of study."[1] By study is meant correspondence courses on the bible. A keen student of the scriptures could in time make progress up a whole hierarchy of examinations and diplomas. "You have to work very hard at it, reading and studying. I've been through all the bible courses. I'm going on to the teachers course soon. That's for Sunday school teachers. I intend to do that when I go out."

But far from promoting cohesion amongst the fundamentalists, the common tasks of study and reflection, the shared aspirations and examinations were a source of friction. "Most of the other people that go to services and do the bible courses, they're the worst people in here. Some of them do the bible courses by cheating. They copy off one another. That's the only way they've got as far as they have. I've written and told the bible school what's going on and as soon as I get out I shall go and tell them personally. I shall expose them," threatened one disgruntled evangelist. "When I leave here I want to go to college and train for the ministry or to be a missionary" he continued.

It was even possible to begin the missionary work right here and now, according to a rather less dedicated devotee. "They can try and persuade other people to turn religious and it makes them feel they've done something useful. Because of what they've done." Just being around in a place like 'A' wing could be part of God's design. "I spend a lot of time with Harry. I know there's a lot of rumours about me and him but I don't take any notice of them. He's had homosexual tendencies in the past and because of that they think he's a bad influence on me. But I've noticed a big change in him in that direction in the last eighteen months. I stay with him really *to bring him grace*." The payoff from all this activity varied from one person to another. For the would-be missionary there was a measure of relief. "When you've done a crime like I've done, you think about it a lot. I've thought about it a lot, especially this last eighteen months since I changed (religion). It was a terrible thing, but I feel better in myself now. I feel more relaxed. I've noticed a change in myself too. I don't swear, and in my attitude to other people I'm better."[2]

But another man, not a religious extremist, who had equally terrible memories to cope with, and who went regularly to 'C of E' services, derived little solace from his attendance. "I can't say it's to bring me peace of mind because it doesn't. I'd be a fool to say it does." For those less anxious about their offences, just going to services did sometimes provide at least a degree of comfort. "I enjoy it because it brings you peace of mind. Reading the bible it helps me. I read certain parts of the bible and I feel better. Matthew 23 are some of my favourite bits. I don't know what it says but I'm always reading it."[3]

Going to chapel, however, confessed one man, was just "something to do on a Sunday; it's a boring day." Like exercise and association; like evening classes and Saturday films, the weekly chapel and other religious activities represent raw materials from which crude aids to the doing of time can be fashioned. Some men clearly used them at that level. Others sought forgiveness. A few fitted them into patterns of homespun, jackdaw philosophising. To the more sceptical amongst the other prisoners however, the antics of the 'faithful' appeared repulsive. "There's a lot of bible punchers here. A lot of hypocrites. They go to all their services but its only to get something for themselves from the people who come in from outside to run them. Singing hymns; I don't know what good that does them." "They're trying to make themselves out to be better than they really are." "I think it's hypocritical, most of them that go, trying to get out of what they've done."

There were at the same time two other and rather weaker religious forces at work on the protection wing. One of them was a minor movement for conversion to the Sikh faith. A man had arrived at Shepton Mallet with a successful conversion to his credit. His cell card was colour coded white for 'other' religion and on it was actually written 'Sikh'. Shortly after his arrival two members of the Celt group applied to re-muster as Sikh. Privately, one of the applicants was quite frank about his motives; "I'm changing religion to Sikh just to have a go back at the bastards. They reckon I'm supposed to have my hair cut every month. Nobody's going to make me have my hair cut every month. Four screws have told me today to have my hair cut. I've told them they can't touch me because I'm changing to Sikh, and they're fucked. I told them I'd get them fucked. I'll do it. If there's a rule I can use to get back at them I will do." He was not too certain about the eventual success of his campaign since Sikhs, he thought, had to wear a knife and a silver ring. The chances of getting either, he estimated, were slim.

Last but not least, a witch was discovered living on the top landing of 'A' wing. Occult signs and writing decorated the walls of his cell. He spoke knowledgeably and seriously about his beliefs. Later, the cell next door was occupied by a younger man, previously unknown to him, who also turned out to be a witch. "Just look about you. Who rules the world? It only makes sense to worship him doesn't it?" demanded the new arrival rhetorically. But when asked about the happy co-incidence of two witches finding themselves in adjoining cells, the younger man was only moderately enthusiastic. "Trouble is with him next door, he's more of a Solomonic Satanist. There's a lot of White Magic mixed up with his stuff. Not in mine though. I'm total black."

Religion in the community of scapegoats then, is not a simple phenomenon. More often divisive than cohesive, it appears to be a personal measure adopted by individuals looking for solutions to the inherent dilemmas of their social situation. In the case of the fundamentalists, the profession of faith fulfilled both retrospective and prospective functions. It offered a chance to come to terms with awful offences, not simply by confession but through hard work. Ordinary prisoners, whether they deny the gravity of their offences or not, can at least offset them to some extent by thinking of their sentences as payment of their 'debt to society'. Forty Threes are hounded out of the relative comfort of that position by their fellow prisoners. They replace it in part with religion.

An additional gain is also possible. "With the Elims you know where you stand", was how one man put it. Moral certainty is an elusive state at the best of times and in the best of places. In prison, men find themselves in a society which has no clear moral basis; a society in which men must fend for themselves as best they can. This uncertainty and unpredictability reduces a man's ability to do his time. Not knowing whether an offence is wiped out in the Great Ledger can be a crippling burden for an offender. Fundamentalist religion provides one kind of answer and one which is strongly suited to the Protestant philosophy of penitentiary prison systems. The quest for certainty and predictability underlies a great part of the collective rules, roles and activities which together constitute the inmate subculture. Denied the few fragile, near certainties that ordinary prisoners have gleaned over the years from their unpromising environment, the Forty Threes have had to invent a few of their own. Extreme religiosity is one such attempt, but cast as it is in the mould of sectarian Protestantism, it remains an intensely personal matter. The articles of the nonconformist faiths affirm that forgiveness must be sought and won in a face to face encounter with the Creator. The personal and restricted nature of such transactions is underlined by the non-appearance of millenial cults in prison communities. Personal revelation, it seems, is a satisfactory alternative to socially concerted action.

Sponsorship

A different and more down to earth way of easing, rather than escaping, the pains of imprisonment was apparent in some of the dealings between Rule Forty Three men. "I was very nervous when I came here first of all. I wouldn't speak to anyone. Then this man sort of took pity on me and talked to me. He's gone out but I'm better now. I can talk to one or two." An unexpected kind of relationship between prisoners is referred to in this statement. It is that of the sponsor; a role which approaches one that can almost be described as that of a 'counsellor'. It is a role which goes beyond that of a mere 'mate'. The sponsor is usually an older and 'prison wiser' inmate who takes under his wing a less experienced, or more socially inept man. He can explain the ways of the prison and help his protegé to do his time 'easy'; or at least with greater ease than he would manage left to his own devices.

Too few instances of the role were observed at Shepton to be able to say whether 'sponsorship' is an important part of prison socialisation or not. And for the most part the cases studied seemed concerned with matters which at first sight do not appear to be of great moment. "With the darts or the table tennis, if you're not very good at scoring they won't let you play. So if you're poor at figures, or you're not very quick, no one will take the chalk for you. I'm not very good at scoring so I usually say 'Reg, will you take the chalk for me?'. And then Freddy likes a game of darts but he's not good at scoring so I'll do it for *him* sometimes. But most of them refuse to let him play. They don't like him anyway." Although the example may appear trivial, the activities during association are amongst the most important occasions when group bonds are likely to emerge, if ever.

To another man the mechanics of chalking up the dart game scores provided an opportunity for more systematic sponsorship. "I talk to him a bit. He's not a bad kid. He came to me and said he was no good at arithmetic. 'Would I help him?' 'Well' I said 'I'll take you on if you promise to keep at it.' And he did. And now he's one of the best scorers on the dartboard. I generally do that for about half a dozen of them."

Sponsorship can extend into two allied activities; 'confession' and 'counselling'. Despite the prohibition on disclosing what one was in for, there was as we have seen, a great deal of rumour and speculation about other people's offences. Bottling up this sort of information about themselves was however impossible for a few men. They *had* to tell somebody about it. A striking and paradoxical example was provided by Burden, the cleaner on the non-Forty Three wing at Shepton, who at a previous prison had played a leading part in the persecution of sex cases. "There was a man worked with me on the pantry there. Everyone thought he was in for thieving but one day he said to me 'Can I tell you something in confidence?' I said 'Yes.' He said 'It's been preying on my mind. I must tell somebody.' It was incest with his sixteen year old daughter. It had been going on since she was fourteen. She wasn't a little girl of five or six. I never told anybody about him." He explained his discreet response by stressing the age of the girl in the case, but in only slightly different circumstances, Burden would have been whispering obscene threats through the Judas hole rather than acting as a confidant.[4]

When a confessional outburst occurs, the chosen listener has to make some definition of his position and decide whether to opt for a greater or lesser degree of involvement in the problems of the other. He may of course just listen. "He told me what he was in for. He seemed to want to and I couldn't stop him. I'm a good listener and it seemed to do him good so I let him get it off his chest." Or more active counselling can take place: "I used to tell him all my troubles. He understood me. He used to say 'Don't hold anything back' and I'd tell him all that I was feeling. It used to do me good." Sometimes 'talkers' failed to select 'listeners' and two men would attempt simultaneously to unburden their own problems on each other.

In another context, elements of religious confession and secular counselling were combined in the weekly meetings of Alcoholics Anonymous. The group was run by an alcoholic prisoner with vigour and ingenuity and it attracted a growing membership. By the time that a quarter of the wing population was attending meetings the staff pressed for a top limit of ten men at any one meeting.[5] Although some of the men who joined AA were obviously and genuinely afflicted by alcoholic problems when outside, there were many others who were not. They were attracted to the meetings by a mixture of utilitarian and personal considerations. On the strictly practical side, it meant extra time out of one's cell over and above the ordinary ration of association. It was also suspected by officers that the cigarettes dispensed by the outside sponsor who came in for the meetings had something to do with the size of the attendance.

But for some who joined, AA clearly represented a secular alternative to extremist religion. It offered an explanatory framework for some of the kinds of unacceptable behaviour in which many of them had engaged. And it offered, again through the medium of confession and hard work, the possibility of moral progress. Since there was nothing in the ordinary regime of the prison which even remotely resembled 'treatment' the men were obviously trying to come to terms with their offences and to repair the damage done to their self esteem by recruitment to Rule Forty Three. It is doubtful that attendance at AA was in fact of much use to the non-alcoholic sex offenders since most of the genuine members tended to be thieves and embezzlers. That meant that all the talk of alcoholism revolved around property offences. Nobody, apparently, was ever able to present to the group an account of his sexual behaviour in terms of alcoholic addiction. By all accounts the sex offenders sat silently listening to the thieves and catching at the 'therapeutic' atmosphere for their own private use.

The absence of any official 'treatment' activities must have contributed to the peer based styles of 'getting by' described in this section. Salvation, sponsorship and attendance at AA meetings involve no contact with uniformed staff, but other modes of adjustment do. Anti-staff sentiment and complaining have already been discussed from the inmate point of view. How the staff perceived their situation at Shepton; the nature of their captives, and the best way of dealing with them must also be examined before any conclusions can be presented about the striking of an equilibrium between the two groups; the men in blue and the men in grey.

Notes

1. Attitudes like this, which were more widespread than the surface com-
posure of some sex offenders suggested, are a neat exposition of the
ideological basis of modern imprisonment.
2. Secular alternatives to repentance and atonement have been so slow to
develop or have been so impractical and expensive (e.g. psychotherapy)
as to be of little use to men serving sentences of imprisonment.
3. "And whosoever shall exalt himself shall be abused and he that shall
humble himself shall be exalted."
"But woe unto you, scribes and Pharisees and hypocrites . . . for ye are
like unto whited sepulchres which indeed appear beautiful outward but
are within full of dead mens' bones and of all unclean-ness." Verses
from Matthew. Chapter 23.
4. See discussion in Chapter 2, Sentence by Ordeal.
5. Officers did not sit in on AA meetings at Shepton, as is the case in some
other prisons, and the growing membership was thought by staff to
represent a 'security threat'. Limits on numbers were also applied to
other non-supervised activities. Because staff drew comfort from a
'tough' definition of their work, trouble free gatherings of large numbers
of prisoners outside of any disciplinary control, represented a threat to
their self esteem and to their bargaining position in regard to wages or
manning levels.

CHAPTER 7

The Haunting of the Screws

The White Lady

Before considering the staff view of things, mention ought to be made of a minor but slightly bizarre event which preceded the transfer of the Forty Three prisoners from Manchester to Shepton Mallet.

In the autumn of 1966 Shepton Mallet was an eerie place. Although the Army had gone for good, it had left behind a lingering reputation for harsh treatment and bad conditions. Hangings and even shootings had allegedly taken place inside its walls and the treadmill had been trodden there within living memory. Towards the end of their tenancy the military had allowed the building to deteriorate. It had been painted at some time from end to end in a bright orange paint. Now it was the worse for wear. It was cold and it was damp. Grass grew between the grey stones of the alleys and steps that linked the yard levels. And it was dark and empty. A working party of 'short-term' prisoners was housed in one corner of one wing but the rest of the place lay silent; not the silence of an ordered nick with every man behind his door and 'All's well with the world', but a heavier and more menacing quality.

Because the working party prisoners were sleeping in, so were the night watch officers; two at a time. One slept at the gate and the other in a small bow fronted room between the empty hall of the chapel and the wing where the men were. One night the duty officer was awakened by something; someone was shaking him by the shoulders. When he came to, he saw that it was a woman in white; a ghostly lady who appeared to walk off

106

through the wall beneath his waking gaze. A disquieting experience. The next night she came again. There was talk of refusing sleep-in duty and the padre was called for, the apparition being thought the responsibility of his department. He refused to exorcise the spectre of the White Lady, as she was by now known. It was just the emptiness of the building, he explained; the power of its past reputation, and a dash of suggestibility. The White Lady did not exist. The moment passed.

Common knowledge in the town, however, confirmed the legend of a White Lady who haunted the prison. Perhaps she was the wife of a past keeper; or even one of the women who had been held in the House of Correction. Might she even be the shade of Jane Brooks; kept there and executed for witchcraft in 1658? Meanwhile the few prisoners living in the prison prayed that she might reappear in their quarters; only more tangibly. The governor, a rational, even a cynical man, resolved to demonstrate that he did not command his staff to sleep where he might fear to, and he arranged to spend a night in the so called 'haunted' room. Halfway through the night he received in the middle of his back a blow of considerable force from something or someone he could not see.

All of this had occurred and been extinguished from everyday recollection before the arrival of the body of Forty Threes from Manchester. In a way it was of prophetic importance and helps to root the Forty Three phenomenon in a long history of scapegoating. Fear of the unknown, the occult obverse of religion, a sexual element; the White Lady might serve as a motif for much of what was to follow. The incident was followed by demands from staff for double manning in every situation which involved actual contact with the protection cases.

Prison Officer Attitudes to Rule Forty Three Men

When a new prison is opened it is Prison Department practice to advertise the officer and trades posts throughout the service nationally, and to invite applications from those serving at other prisons. A self-selected staff group is more likely to appear therefore in a new prison than in an established one where change is slow and involuntary postings are more common. Prisoners believed that hundreds of 'screws' had applied for posts at Shepton Mallet in the firm belief that a Rule Forty Three prison would mean twenty-three hours a day in solitary confinement for the prisoners on protection. Such a prison would, to many officers, including some who found their way to Shepton, represent a return to the 'good old days'. "That's how I like to see it" said a long-serving officer one night after lock-up at eight o'clock. "All behind their doors, neat and tidy. That's what I call a proper nick."

Unfortunately for him and his scheme of things, and for other officers like him, the official policy for Rule Forty Threes at Shepton was that prisoners should lead a 'normal' prison life; working together and associating as freely as they would were they not 'on protection'. Even less happily for them, the first governor of the prison interpreted this brief with a liberal vigour which affronted their deepest held notions of institutional justice.

Any systematic gathering of staff opinion had been forbidden by the Home Office, so this part of the material is drawn from informal observation of everyday situations. Scrutiny of the notes recording observed incidents and casual conversations with officers yields up one word and one dimension relating to staff—inmate interaction which is clearly of overwhelming importance to them. The word is 'give' and the dimension is one of 'giving' and 'withholding'. Men in prisons have few rights they can insist upon, but most regimes possess a range of exchange items which are termed 'privileges', Wages, association with others, recreation facilities, and token improvements to the standard of living, constitute the stock of rewards available in most jails. More substantial carrots like early release on parole, working-out schemes or extra visits, are all held in reserve and are negotiable only when the prisoner has accumulated considerable good behaviour credits. The minor privileges, however, are usually granted all at once, to all inmates, and the threat of their withdrawal is used as a control measure.

Between these two extremes there is a zone of privileges and rewards which lie within the discretion of staff. Sought-after job assignments are controlled by basic grade and slightly more senior staff. Other discretionary items to do with leisure activities or communication with the outside world are in the gift of the governor. The queue for governor's application, a daily right for serving prisoners, is frequently filled by men in search of some small favour from the administration. In the eyes of prison officers, Rule Forty Three cases are paradigm losers in this struggle for scarce resources. They do not qualify for even the tiniest increments of status, power or possession. They should exemplify a total poverty and complete absence of power and privilege which is rightly the fate of the unworthy and the unco-operative. The fact that Forty Threes are created, not by fiat of the system, but by the voluntary activity of the inmate group is, from the standpoint of the 'screws', an additional bonus.

When Forty Threes at Shepton then, in keeping with the policy of the place, were given ordinary prison privileges, the staff saw it as an extraordinary denial of the principle of desert. "They go into the governor here and they get everything they ask for. They ought to have to earn it the hard way; not just get it given to them", said one officer. How they were to 'earn' their privileges was not clear since they were by common consent a passive and docile group; offering good behaviour spontaneously and requiring little in the way of either coercion or of reward. In fact, staff thought the Forty Three men should be denied privileges, not because of what they did or did not do in prison, but because of what they were; convicted sex offenders in the main.

The whole principle of giving and withholding and the satisfactions it offered to the staff was illustrated during a meeting of the Home Leave Board. A senior officer, the chaplain and the welfare officer considered applications from all men serving three years and over who qualified for a few days home leave during the last few months of their sentences. Men with wives or parents who were willing to receive them back usually went through with little difficulty, unless they had been troublesome to staff, or the probation officer outside had reported adversely on home conditions. Solitary men with no homes to go to and no ties with any particular place were more problematical. Their names were automatically submitted to the Prison Department for comment in addition to any purely local or practical considerations.

When 'Quasimodo' (see p. 79, Chapter 4, The Shape of the Community) appeared before the Home Leave Board, he had been referred back by Head Office as a poor risk who should not be allowed out until his full term expired. Before the man was called in to hear the decision there was some discussion by the Board members about how the news should be broken to him. The senior officer, who acted as chairman, proposed to tell the man that since he could not himself suggest an address where he might go, his application had been unsuccessful. In reply to the suggestion that he could just report a Head Office refusal of permission and that his own proposed explanation would lead the prisoner to blame him personally for the decision, the officer said: "I don't mind what these people think of me. As long as you're doing something for them you're a good bloke. But as soon as you don't give them something, you're every kind of bastard under the sun. I don't want these bastards to like me. I don't like them. I think as little of them as they think of me. It's moments like this that make this job worthwhile. When you can tell 'em 'no'."

The open-handed pattern of privilege granting which prevailed in the prison also seemed to have control implications for another officer: "There's no discipline. When these Forty Threes came here they were like sheep to the slaughter. You could do anything with them. They'd do everything you told them. That was because the prisons where they'd come from, they'd been treated hard. After about a month they saw they were getting everything, and they started getting cocky. Then they started complaining about everything and putting in petitions all the

time. Far in excess of what they did at other prisons. They
should have been slapped down at the start then it wouldn't
have gone on. They ought to be treated just the same as
any other prisoners. That's what I thought when I came here.
Trouble is they're getting treated far better than other prisoners.
I think its failed. Now they don't think they're getting privileges;
they think they're rights."

The question of control is a crucial one which will be discussed below, but what this officer said clearly establishes a
staff view of the Forty Threes as a 'complaining' group. "This
lot here, spineless lot of gits, always moaning, always complaining. I wouldn't mind that if they came up and did it to
your face, but they don't", said another junior officer. "There's
one or two you can talk to, but all the rest, they're just grasses."
In other words staff could not feel safe in saying anything in
front of Forty Threes for fear of it being passed on. Behind that
feeling lies another set of implicit assumptions about the mutual
interdependence of convicts and lower echelon staff.

Officers' judgements about the moral qualities of 'A' wing
inmates also extended into generalised feelings about their
physical appearance. "Anywhere else they look like ordinary
people but these are a poor lot." "Look at this lot; they look
weedy and bedraggled." "What a dirty, scruffy, disreputable
lot." "They look unhealthy and degraded and disgusting and
dirty and unfit." From such feelings about the nature of their
charges, it was only a short step to defining the whole Shepton
Mallet situation as alien to their self-identifications as prison
officers. "I don't call this lot proper prisoners." "I don't call
this a prison at all." "I don't call this a proper prison." "I don't
call this proper prison work." "It'd be a relief to get to
Dartmoor. You've got some real prisoners there."

Some of this feeling was ascribed by officers to a general
lack of 'busyness' at Shepton Mallet. They claimed to be anxious
to transfer to other prisons, proper prisons where their pro-
motion prospects would not be in jeopardy. It seemed almost
as though they were afraid that the taint of the Rule might rub
off on them; blighting their occupational futures and even

wreaking havoc with their manhood. In 'normal' prisons staff can combat the threat of corruption from the outlaws they guard by constant reference to their violent and dangerous nature and to the toughness of their job. At Shepton, staff would reminisce about real prisoners, tough guys, they had known previously in other prisons. "Frankie Fraser; what a load of shit. Hard as fucking iron. You could hit him with a stick, kick him; he wouldn't bat an eyelid." "Do you remember carrying guns there (at Dartmoor) right up to 1952?"

Staff Cohesion

Despite the widely held nature of these and similar sentiments there was not much evidence of staff solidarity. There was in fact evidence to the contrary. Prisoners who worked close to officers in positions of trust frequently mentioned the absence of loyalties amongst the staff. They would retail personal gossip and sexual scandal about fellow officers in front of men who grew frankly contemptuous of them. And officers themselves expressed sentiments about the competence of higher ranking officers as well as dissatisfaction with the whole staff scene: "You wouldn't believe the petty jealousy that goes on in a small place like this. You just wouldn't believe how childish the officers get towards one another. The trouble is you know everybody else and you know just what duty they're on. So they come in in the morning and look at the duty list. They say 'Oh look what so and so's got and look what I've got' and then they're moaning and complaining. I can't stand it."

But it does not follow from this catalogue of dissensions that the staff at Shepton was incapable of cohesion on any subject They were largely united, as we have seen, in their dislike of the Rule Forty Three prisoners. They closed ranks too against the possibility of intrusion by outsiders into their closed world; a world which they saw defended by the fundamental smells of slopping out and the easily mistaken nature of the occasional violence they thought necessary for control. "It's not right bringing outsiders onto the wing" said one long serving officer. "I'm not against classes and that sort of thing, but in the proper place, outside the wing. You shouldn't bring people in where they're living. Especially women. You get them carrying pots around; slopping out. They don't want to see that. And they might see things they shouldn't. If one of the men turns nasty and he has to be put into a cell, well, they shouldn't see that. They might not understand. Someone's got to do it. The welfare people won't do it; they'll turn tail and run. Well, things go on that people shouldn't see. Or they might get involved. Then there'll be questions for letting someone unauthorised get into a position where they can get hurt."

Persistent and inquiring visitors to the prison were commonly held to be inspired by what some officers called 'morbid curiosity'. Survivors from the silent age of prisons were particularly prone to these doubts about outsiders. It is a tribute to the chilling nature of their inherited reputation that many prisons are indeed visited by people who are motivated by a curiosity that is patently and openly morbid.

A further occasion for the cultivation of 'we-feeling' amongst the staff was provided by the changing of the shifts. At the end of the day shift, all the outgoing officers assembled in the gate lodge. Instead of leaving as they arrived in ones, twos and threes from the four corners of the prison, they waited until the whole shift was packed into the tiny lobby between the inner security door and the outer gate. Technically the reason for this was that keys could more easily be collected and visually checked on the key board if the entire shift was present. Ordinarily this process took up to ten minutes to complete, and non-uniformed staff who arrived at the gate during that time were trapped along with the others until all the keys were accounted for. The whole proceedings were marked by explosive hilarity and ribaldry; part of it looking back on the happenings of the prison day; part of it anticipating the pleasures of the free time just about to begin. The effect to the onlooker was rather like that of a collection of deep sea divers coming up for air and pausing just below the surface in an airlock to allow the bubbles in the bloodstream to disperse. Locked in between the inner and outer skins of the prison wall the officers were effectively in a role changing room where the tensions and the pressures of the work were exchanged for more relaxed leisure roles.

One other thing which united many of the uniformed members of staff was their condemnation of work carried out in the welfare office of the prison. For a start they saw it as a disturbing influence in the delicate pattern of giving and withholding. "There's two sides to the prison, the discipline and the welfare side. I personally think its gone too far in that direction." Since the whole operating philosophy of Shepton Mallet was already deeply offensive to staff notions, the presence of a welfare function was doubly irritating. Particular concern was apparent over the right of the welfare office to sanction extra 'privileges' like letters or visits. Even the spending of time on this man or that was looked on with suspicion; so strong was the staff feeling that prisoners should all be treated exactly the same. One officer carried this principle to its negative extreme: "I never read their records. If I knew what they're in for I wouldn't be able to treat 'em fair. I'd probably want to strangle 'em. I've got kids of my own."

Mostly though, the officers were concerned that a gullible welfare officer, unversed in the ways of the prison, was an easy mark for the prisoners who wished to 'con' some privilege from him. And to emphasise the point, they repeated whenever possible, expressions of ingratitude made by prisoners concerning the efforts of welfare officers. "These bastards aren't grateful for anything you do. Do you know what they say about you behind your back? They come out saying 'Fucking waste of time going to see him. He's done fuck all for me.' " "Nobody here appreciates what you are doing." "Do you think any of them appreciate what you do for them one little bit? They're just out to get what they can out of you." "They think they'll by-pass the Principal Officer or the Chief and ask you to give them something." "With all respect to you, you people are very easily conned into these things."[1]

Another aspect of staff antipathy to welfare was their fear

that it might promote rather than stifle the whining complaints of the Rule Forty Threes and it was also seen as personally unpleasant work. "I can talk to some of them some of the time, but most of them, eeugh. I just couldn't do the job." I couldn't be a welfare officer. It's bad enough telling them what to do, without having to talk to them as well."

The most useful informant on this topic was a former prison officer then serving a prison sentence and who was on protection from his former captives. He summarised the clash between control and welfare ideologies in the prison like this: "Officers get it dinned into them during training 'you must be fair', 'you must be straight'. Officers think you give cons too much. They've been taught that the rule is you give one letter a week, one visit a month and that's it. Anything else, you're *giving* to them. It's a privilege. You must know they con you all the time. They're only out for what they can get. All officers are at war with welfare officers. I've never known one that was really liked by the screws. They don't belong. They're nobody's people." Oppositon to welfare's debasement of the currency of privilege did not stop at words. Extra letters and visits sanctioned by the welfare office were sometimes ignored, obstructed and sabotaged in a variety of ways. At its most gentle it took the form of reproofs, raised eyebrows or statements about being conned. But some letters were not issued, and visits could be delayed or restricted in ways which destroyed their value.

One major facet of staff pre-occupations has been left for the next section, and that is the question of control; not just in terms of head-on confrontation, but a subtler business involving differential responses from officers as well as prisoners. So far, the most striking thing to emerge about the staff at Shepton Mallet is their similarity in some respects to the men in their charge; socially isolated;[2] internally divided; bitterly critical of their superiors; scornful of the opposition but haunted by fears of contamination; and insistent on absolute equality and fairness of treatment to the point of knowing nothing about anybody. A prisoner well qualified by long experience to judge such matters said; "I reckon the staff at Shepton are all rejects from the other prisons. They're all the old stagers that nobody else wants. They just don't compare with the screws at any other prison I've been to." And another asked: "What did they want to come here for? It's a crummy nick in a crummy part of a crummy town in the middle of nowhere. They're on Rule Forty Three themselves."

Notes

1. Some of the prisoners were as eager as the staff to disabuse the Welfare Officer of any ideas of utility. After the departure of one long sentence man with whom I had spent a lot of time and with whom I enjoyed "a good relationship" the man in the next cell to him was keen to pass on his departed friend's epitaph on my efforts. "That welfare officer", he is reported to have said, "he ain't worth half a wank".
2. During the Army's occupation of Shepton Mallet a large self-contained housing estate had been built for the soldiers to the south of the town. Although the houses were generally inferior in size and quality to those normally provided for prison officers, the principle of a separate estate on the fringes of the town was not new to them. Like other social dirty-workers, officers are expected, and to an extent themselves expect, to have to live in isolated ghettoes. Although this has the effect of separating prison officers physically and socially from the surrounding population it does not necessarily lead to greater internal cohesion. It may even have the opposite effect by creating the kind of claustrophobia and tension common to island or mountain communities, to garrisons, and to ships' crews.

CHAPTER 8

'Screws and Cons'; Striking a Balance

Re-defining Reality

"You'd never catch me going to an officer and sticking my nose right up his arse. I keep right away from them." These words are a crude précis of the most prevalent attitude expressed by Forty Threes towards the staff at Shepton Mallet. Avoiding any kind of involvement with officers, either by engaging them voluntarily in conversation or by behaving in any way which might attract their attention, was widely held to be an ideal way of doing 'quiet' time. It is the same attitude in fact as the one held towards relations between convicts themselves. It implies a 'cool' and self-controlled performance in the face of even quite severe provocation. "If they get a bit stroppy, I obey" said one man. "I don't make a scene about it. Like last night I was just getting some water and the officer was trying to get through early and he shouted at me. But I didn't answer him back. *You take one of them on and you might as well take on the whole prison of them.* They all stick together. That's why I never try it." As a way of getting by in total and totalitarian institutions, displays of passive conformity have an apparently universal application. Life in an Eastern European army was just like an English prison, according to a man with experience of both. "I was in the Army there seven years. I never have no trouble. I just say 'Yes sir, No sir' and never get any trouble. Do the same here." Superficial compliance can however mask contrary but privately held definitions of the situation. "I get on well with the officers, but just so far. I do what they tell me and I'm polite but I do it because I want to do it, and I don't want to

lose time. *And I'll do the work in my own time.* It shows them
I'm willing but I'm not going down on my knees to them." In
other words, whatever his outward appearance may be, this
prisoner retains, in his own imagination at least, a measure of
control over the events in which he is involved. He invests his
activities with qualities of autonomy and personal dignity,
which, since they are not normally put on show cannot be
attacked or diminished by others.

In his account of concentration camp life in Dachau, Bruno
Bettelheim draws attention to the exceptional morale and
behaviour of the Jehova's Witnesses.[1] When all about them were
acting like animals they almost alone retained their moral convictions. Assuming that Witnesses do not recruit disproportionate
numbers of supermen one can only surmise that their ability to
survive the dreadful privations of Dachau was due to the
strength of their ideology. The most salient of their beliefs is
that we live in the immediately pre-Apocalyptic era, and that
the second coming of Christ is imminent. One of the prophesied
symptoms of this era is the persecution of God's people so that,
to the Witnesses, the ghastly experience of Dachau could be
seen as the working out of God's purpose; therefore predictable
and to some extent bearable.

For ideologically less-well-equipped prisoners, personally
entertained definitions merge into fantasies which are more
explicit but less peaceable. One overtly quiet and well-behaved
prisoner said: "There are cons that will have a go at officers.
Get 'em down on the ground and kick their faces in. So their
mouths are all kicked in and their eyes all pushed in. Even kick
their eyes out." The likelihood of him ever personally engaging
in such bloody behaviour is remote. Only one or two men
openly advocated such active resistance. A member of the Celt
group said for example: "What we could do with here is a riot.
That would ginger things up a bit. I'd start one if I could but
there aren't enough people here to back it up. They haven't got
the guts. They haven't got the bottle."[2] In view of the lack of
potential support from his fellow prisoners he probably felt safe
in making such brave statements, but he was not the only

person with an interest in the subject. Talking about riots and developing scenarios about how the staff would handle them was a favoured pastime for the Forty Threes. A particularly intriguing question was how individual officers would react to a riot and especially what they would do with their riot sticks. There were prisoners who claimed that senior officers had confessed to them that in the event of a mutiny they would jettison their sticks through the window into the yard to avoid the possibility of being beaten by them.

The trouble with a riot though, is the extent and intensity of the co-operative behaviour necessary to sustain it. Prisoners were sceptical that such co-operation could ever take place. Open defiance, protest or hostility becomes therefore a thing for individual expression.

Sometimes this can be combined in a harmless way with a prisoner's private definitions of personal dignity: "I knew a bloke at Scrubs who used to make a majestic thing out of slopping out. He was a big, tall feller and he used to wrap a blanket round him like a cloak and walk along all erect. Really majestic it was." Few men in prison possess either the sense of drama or the self-confidence to express themselves like that man. Alternative forms of symbolic protest are however available; protest that is combined with attempts to exert control over the environment and to increase the predictability of staff behaviour.

The links between the symbolic inner world inhabited by an individual and the real world in which he lives are not easy to elucidate. Some prisoners entertain private thoughts about getting their own back on the system. Occasionally these are translated into action by the individual concerned or by someone with whom he may identify. But applause for the man who puts such thoughts into words or deeds is often tempered with criticism to the effect that giving vent to his private fantasies is an indulgence for which the group he belongs to must pay the price. An attack on one officer, as one man said, is an attack on them all. Conversely from the staff standpoint, an attack by one prisoner is an attack by them all. Although the doctrine of col-

lective responsibility is not spelled out to civil prison populations, as it was, say, in concentration camps, and an official
philosophy of social isolationism is urged on the men, there is
no doubt that restrictions are often placed on the many because
of fears about the few.

So when a man can no longer contain his feelings and he
snaps back at an officer or raises his fist he becomes at the same
time both a hero of sorts, and a saboteur of the status quo. The
same applies to complainers and petitioners. They give voice to
what others are thinking but fear to say lest they make things
worse. Persistent complainers are pleaded with: "People sometimes say to me 'do your time' but to me that's a defeatist
policy. I ruck about everything. They can't brainwash me", in
this case to little effect; but it is essential that at least a fraction
of the complaints are communicated to the officials if their
behaviour is to be influenced at all. It is part of the condition
of powerlessness that impotent fantasy is all that the deprived
can aspire to, and ironical that its acting out is constrained by
the fears of the like minded for the consequences. It was plain
to one man that: "The people who complain the most get the
worst treatment."

The Posthumous Threat

A nice illustration of the nervous and symbolic nature of
mutual constraint between prisoners and officers is the frequent
use by Forty Threes of what may be called 'the posthumous
threat'. Basically this took the form of promised retaliation,
scheduled to take place after the release of the speaker. Some
posthumous threats were purely mental events and concerned
previous situations, the offence, being shopped, being let down.
And in those cases where the assumed transgressors were still
outside or had left prison it made sense to think of retribution
at a future date.[3] "When I was walking round on Forty Three
exercise one day a dirty slag started to call me from a cell
window. He was yelling dirty things about my wife. He said:

'Your wife's a ride.' He knew I couldn't get at him, but if I see him outside I'll kill him: the dirty slag." "He did a dirty trick on me. And my mum. I might see him outside."

But where the threatened person is presently available 'postponement' serves another function. In the case of threats against officers, which were numerous, the 'posthumous' element in the postponement of execution was clearly intended to achieve an effect in terms of staff behaviour, whilst avoiding the dangers of an actual confrontation or attack here and now. Most of the threats were issued well away from the hearing of the threatened person. A very few were made face to face, and some were transmitted to the staff by other inmates. The threats themselves take a constant and economically brief form, as in this example: "That fucking PO. He's doing me down deliberately. Well, I'll remember that. I'll be down round this way when I've been released and I'll make him sorry. I'll remember." Usually nothing is specifically promised beyond 'seeing' the person involved, but the unspoken message is that he will be beaten up, or damage done to his family or sometimes, interestingly enough, to his car. Rule Forty Three cases are not the only prisoners who engage in 'posthumous threats'; they are endemic to the prison system, but only occasionally is a threat actually carried out against an officer or his family outside. The rarity with which they are executed does not diminish their obvious general utility as a control agency when diffused into the everyday consciousness of the staff.

It would be difficult to make any measurement of the extent to which Rule Forty Three men rely on private definitions and posthumous threats, and to compare them with other kinds of prisoners or different regimes. Probably both mechanisms would be found in all prisons, but concentrated more significantly amongst the most isolated and powerless prisoners. Long-term prisoners, whether they draw support from the inmate subculture or not, are also more likely than short-termers to engage in these forms of behaviour since they must spread their self-control so thinly over so many years. A long sentence, to many men, represents a siege-like assault on their consciousness and their self-respect. Sitting it out is one style of 'getting by' in this situation and it means not yielding to urges that counsel defiance or futile gestures of oppositions to the staff.

Evidence about the distribution of conformist attitudes presented in Chapter 5 implied that anti-staff feeling is a one-dimensional phenomenon. Individuals were placed along a continuum from low to high conformity. To the extent that some statistically significant relationships were discovered between those scores and other items it could be argued that they reflect an aspect of reality. On the other hand they artificially simplify what is actually a complex inter-relationship of attitude and activity; and one which is hardly so clear in practice as in the abstracted form of questionnaire scores.

Officer Roles

There were, it is true, individuals on protection who held generalised attitudes about *all* staff. Good ones: e.g. "I think this is a lovely nick. It hasn't got that cloud about it. The atmosphere's good. The officers are good, you can talk to them. I can talk to all of them." And bad ones; "There's only one good screw and that's a dead one. There's none of them any good."

But most of the men were able to make clear distinctions between officers and the way in which they acted towards inmates. They distinguished in fact, four basic role options for officers:

1. the 'bent' screw
2. the 'soft' screw
3. the 'fair' screw;
4. the 'bastard'.[4]

The 'bent' screw is one who has been recruited by prisoners to assist in their illicit enterprises. He acts as a courier, carrying messages, money and other contraband items both into and out of the prison. For his part he may at first be well paid, although once begun, the 'bent' screw is an easy mark for progressive blackmail. Normally the inmate group that recruits him will guard his identity jealously for fear of losing him. And for the inmate group he serves a double function: he helps some of them overcome some of the deprivations they suffer; and he also confirms a universally held piece of prison mythology that 'every man has his price'. To his colleagues on the other hand the 'bent' screw represents an extreme case of alienation. His place amongst his staff peers is, if detected, identical to that of the 'grass' amongst the prisoners. At Shepton Mallet there was little in the way of organised 'fiddles' apart from a bit of betting and some private borrowings of 'snout' and only one claim was ever made, in my hearing that a 'bent' officer existed there. There was of course no evidence that the claim was true, but 'bent' screws do exist and they constitute one logical category in the inmate's role scheme.

Then there is the 'soft' screw. He does not engage in trafficking but simply appears to lack the minimum personal qualities which secure respect, compliance or obedience from the men. 'Soft screws' do not possess what military and para-military organisations call 'leadership quality', or the ability to 'handle men'. From the inmates' point of view, relations with 'soft' officers are pleasantly relaxed, except when senior or more stringent officers are present: "With that screw you know he won't book you whatever you do. As long as you play the game in front of the governor, he's not worried. Normally you can just run off the party and say 'I'm going so-and-so' as you go past him. But when the governor's there, you go up and ask him properly, and he's alright with you the rest of the time." 'Soft' officers are usually liked but not respected and they are complied with in a tactically selective way so as to maximise the benefits of their laxity.

Thirdly there is the 'fair' officer. Basically he upholds the legitimacy of the formal system but comes to terms with prisoners by processes of compromise and accommodation. The 'fair' screw cannot be bought, but he turns a blind eye in the direction of certain rule infractions in return for a necessary level of co-operation. He also displays a predictable kind of integrity and a willingness to overcome obstacles in order that individual inmates shall receive what is due to them. A majority of the prisoners placed a majority of officers into the category of 'fair' screw. They described 'fair' screws as personally amenable: "I get on alright with all the officers. Most of them treat you right. They treat you like you're something. They don't talk to you like you're a dog or a pig." "Most of the officers are real gentlemen. A gentleman's one who treats you like a human being; one that you can talk to and have a laugh and a joke with." And 'fair' screws were seen as being scrupulous in the allocation of benefits: "You can have respect for some screws for the way they treat you. If you're entitled to something they'll go out of their way to make sure you get it. They won't give you things you're not entitled to, but if you are, you get it. That's what I call fair." "He's a good one. If he says it, he means it and he'll push the Chief on one side to get it for you, if you're entitled to it. If you don't qualify, he'll just tell you 'no.' " But the 'fair' screw is not all one sided. He is also engaged in the application of the standing orders and prison rules. "Now there's a lovely officer. He's strictly to the book. You know just where you stand. You can have a laugh and a joke with him but if he says 'do up your button', you do it because you know he means it. He makes sure you get what you're entitled to; by the book, and no more."

There is a fine line which divides the 'fair' screw from the final option, the 'bastard', and it is a matter of personal judgement on the part of convicts into which category a particular officer is to be placed. "I suppose most screws are what you'd call fair", said one man. "You can have a chat with them. Then there's 'bastards'. 'Bastards' just come and give you orders and shout at you. They were like that at Wandsworth. 'Do this' and you'd do it. 'Do that' and you'd do it. Then they'd hurry you up. You never spoke to them. They never spoke to you. Just gave you orders."

The worst thing about the 'bastard' is the way he is "always on to you", "always having a go at you". One officer in particular at Shepton Mallet attracted the 'bastard' label from the Forty Threes because of his physical and challenging approach. "That bloke, he's nothing but an animal. He walks along behind people and nudges them and then says 'Watch it.' He was saying to someone 'Go on, pin one on me' and pushing out his jaw." "They try to push you into doing something back then they can nick you. They say 'The first thing you do I'm going to nick you.' There are only one or two like that here." "Of course there's the odd one that's a pure 'bastard'. There's one here. He's so ignorant. He goes round swearing at everyone and then the minute someone swears back he nicks them. He really is a 'bastard'." And besides being deliberately provocative 'bastards' could also be patronising. "They talk to you like you're just little children. They say "Come along lads, let's get some work done.' There's one of them says that and I'm old enough to be his father." 'Bastards' could make life difficult in other ways as well. "Some screws go out of their way to make things difficult for you like when you've got a 'turnover'.[5] Well, some officers they're in and out because they know you've got nothing. But some of them they turn everything over. Move every little thing. They know there's nothing there but they do it just to make things awkward for you."

Along with all these bad qualities, however, the 'bastard' possesses one saving virtue, that of consistency and predictability. A typical testimony to this quality ran as follows: "I'd rather have a nickful of 'bastards', at least you know where you stand. Rather that than a nickful of 'soft' screws who might suddenly change their minds one day."

Conversely, fears were frequently expressed about the possibility of changing and unpredictable responses by some officers. "Some of them bring their own worries to work with them. They get out of bed the wrong side or have a row with their missus and when they get here they take it out on some poor prisoner. Take Billy. I've seen him on his party tell the screw not to be a silly C. U. N. T. or to 'fuck off' and the screw's smiled; taken it as a joke. Next day he's said the same thing and the screw's had something else on his mind and nicked him for it."

Achieving predictability

The strategies which have been described here; avoidance, private definition, the posthumous threat, and role typing are all predominantly internalised methods for coming to terms with an almost impossible social situation: They rely for their effectiveness on the re-arrangement of external elements into a personally fabricated and therefore personally acceptable version of reality. But they also have practical consequences, in that properly used, they increase the predictability of events and therefore ease the passage of time. In terms of the social types distinguished by Schrag these techniques are most likely to be employed by the straight men or 'square johns' and by the 'right guys' or professionally oriented thieves. Both types have half a mind focused on the outside world. 'Merchants' or con-men and 'outlaws' on the other hand are more likely to respond to the here and now, with manipulation and violence respectively.

Manipulation involves making and maintaining contact with staff members, usually by taking jobs in 'trusted' positions, as cleaners, storemen, clerks etc. Working for the official organisation offers access to many time-beating resources; material benefits like food or clothes, status, and most importantly an ear to the official keyhole. Prior knowledge of forthcoming events is an asset beyond price in the struggle for predictability.

On the practical side, with food for instance, 'trusties' find themselves bound by the same constraints which the prison group brings to bear upon the staff proper. Ironically, as Mathiesen has pointed out, rule-bound bureaucracies provide ready made rods for their own backs. Anyone who knows the rule book can bring pressure upon the system to conform more closely to its provisions. The legend of the barrack room lawyer has grown up in this rich soil. Hoist, as it were, by their own paper work petards, bureaucracies have taken evasive action. They develop dual sets of rules or codes of practice. One set is made public but is carefully constructed to incorporate ambiguities which can only be resolved by reference to secret codes, guides or rulings which are left firmly beneath the counter. In some systems, no such discretion is formally admitted at all and exists on an informal basis which remits even more power to the officials. In prison there are the published rules, and there are unpublished memoranda and standing orders; and both of them define areas of staff discretion where the rules confine, but do not exactly dictate the kinds of decisions or outcomes which are possible. Prisoners can exert a variety of pressures over these discretionary areas as well as on the general behaviour of the staff. The most direct of them is straightforward confrontation based on an open appeal to higher authority. "That officer, when I came here first of all, I thought 'What a pig', but now he's as good as gold. Just after I came here he came along and swore at me. He said 'Get in your effing cell.' I went after him and I said 'Excuse me. What did you say?' He said: 'Mind your own effing business.' I said: 'Don't you swear at me. I just won't have it.' I went straight down and asked the PO to stop his officer from swearing at me. Since then I've had no trouble from him."

If complaints are taken further, formalised or incorporated into petitions the complainer enters very tricky territory. It is an offence against discipline to make false accusations against an officer. And even if the identity of the officer is implied rather than stated openly, the risk of retaliation is still considerable. "On Saturday morning I wrote to my MP about conditions in the shop", said the wing's premier complainer. "On Saturday night I get this. (Three days loss of remission, seven days loss of association, for leaving association without permission.) Anybody else they'd just get a warning. They got me because I complained so much. A lot of cons would like to complain but daren't. They just moan amongst themselves. They think the screws will make life more difficult for them." Despite this man's awareness that his present misfortune was a consequence of his complaints, he promised continuing recourse to the rules. "They want to play it by the book. Well I can play it by the book too." As an example he instanced his registration as a vegetarian, which gave him endless opportunities to fault the administration. Failures to maintain complete segregation between the two wings in the prison were also seen as a challenge to his petitioning ability, although he was not over-optimistic about his chances of success: "I've put in thirteen petitions and I've won two. That's not a bad number. Most of the time you can't win. But it's still worth it. It keeps them on their toes.

A more active but at the same time more covert kind of obstruction was provided by a wing orderly who resented the criticism and carping of the officer supervising the day's cleaning. " 'What about the bridge?' he kept saying.[6] So I just went and threw my brush into the cell. And then I just went brushing slowly round the landing. Nothing got done and when it got to inspection time a lot of it still wasn't done. After that he didn't bother us again."

Outright opposition was rare almost to the point of uniqueness but it brought its own rewards. "I can't stand that screw. Always getting on to you about one thing or another. Always on your back. One day I wasn't feeling too good. There was some trouble at home. So I told him to stick it. I was three days down the block. I thought it was going on for ever." Physical violence was even rarer and an officer, in an unguarded moment, recalled what happened to a 'madman' who struck out and hit a member of the staff. "There was a fight on the threes between two of the blokes. John G. (another officer) went to break it up and Bell hit him twice with a shoe. He said it was an accident. Well, once might be an accident, but not twice. Bell was mad. They certified him and took him off. Some of us gave him a leathering for it afterwards."

Somewhere between the two positions of general conformity and occasional opposition, an uneasy line of mutual staff—inmate accommodation has to be drawn. Its location and stability will depend on the balance, at any particular time, between the varied role types present on both sides, and the particular strategies which they choose to pursue at different times. In the polarised social situation of the prison, and probably in any correctional situation, where one group is designated the 'goodies' and the other the 'baddies', the possibilities of ordinary interaction between them are plainly limited. Two types of extraordinary interaction are however posssible in its place. One of them is the officially prescribed one of orders and obedience, and the other is, corruption. Between these two extremes lies a twilight world where apparent obedience merges imperceptibly with extremely subtle forms of corruption.[7] It is an unstable mixture but most of the time it serves its purpose which is that of striking a balance between the contradictory and seemingly irreconcilable differences that divide the captors from their captives.

Notes

1. Bruno Bettelheim, *The Informed Heart*, The Free Press, Glencoe, 1960.
2. This man did claim to have successfully initiated a mass complaint by men in the metal reclamation shop about working conditions, but he complained bitterly that when in front of the Governor all the fire had gone out of their protest. Shortly after the opening of the prison, but before the period when the study data was collected, a sit down strike actually took place in the workshop. Several factors probably account for this unique event. Amongst the initial shipment of men from Manchester there were a few who were subsequently given 'A' and 'B' security gradings as potential escapees and removed to more secure prisons.

    At Manchester, quite pleasant work had been undertaken making and painting toys and the change to the dirty, noisy futility of cable stripping must have been marked.
3. The 'posthumous threat' is a mechanism with a long pedigree amongst the dispossessed. Millenarian fantasies represent a highly organised version of it which envisage prevailing master—slave relations being totally upturned and reversed. Children, the elderly and the sick may all use it, and suicide itself, if successful, is its ultimate form. "Then you'll be sorry when I'm dead" is a more subtle and circuitous get-back than overt threats of future violence, but it is in the same class of activity.
4. There is a magnetic quality about offenders which make them the exclusive centre of attention of any study of crime or corrections. Victimology, although it enjoyed some vogue during the nineteenth century, has been neglected until recent years. In part this is the result of theoretical perspectives which stressed a genetic or disease origin of crime rather than a social one. Prison staff have suffered from the same neglect.

5. Periodic, random searches of cells designed to uncover illicit possessions, escape material, etc.
6. A catwalk connecting the top landings, halfway along the wing.
7. The dangers of corruption are not of course restricted to those who have power or influence; they are a common hazard for 'helpers' of all kinds and also for researchers, particularly those who adopt a participative style of observation. A common defence employed by researchers who fear identification with their subjects, is a sturdy dedication, at the front of the final report, to the author's wife and children "without whose support this work would not have been possible". See Laud Humphries, *Tea-room Trade, op. cit.* These dangers are particularly pronounced for students who owe allegiance to the 'deviance' approach in sociology; a tradition which asserts that there is much to be learned about a society by squinting up its backside. It is clearly a posture which demands a certain agility on the part of the observer.

CHAPTER 9

Casting the Blame

It is not proposed to attempt here a summary of this account of Rule Forty Three men at Shepton Mallet. Its aim has been to provide a description rather than prove a point or develop even a partial theory of prison. And because it has focused on the Forty Threes only after their recruitment to the Rule, and their subsequent constitution as a separate group, it has not so far addressed itself directly to some of the intriguing questions it is possible to ask concerning their relationship to the prison system as a whole. What function does the scapegoating of these men serve for the main prisoner group for example? And why is the phenomenon apparently on the increase? Since none of the work reported here was done on the problem at its place of origin, in the prisons of reception in England and Wales, only tentative answers can be proposed to these and other questions.

To begin to make sense of the process it may be useful first of all to step back from the immediate issue and to look more widely at the place which prisons presently occupy in modern industrial societies.

Imprisonment as a routine way of dealing with serious offenders is historically recent, and its use on a large scale in this country dates from the almost literal dissolution of the prison hulks resting on the Thames and elsewhere. In a previous era the prison had been primarily a kind of judicial waiting room, where suspects and accused persons were herded together to await 'delivery' by the judge for trial; or where debtors waited for someone to buy them out.[1] For those who were 'delivered' the future lay between stark alternatives; to be freed if found not guilty; or, if convicted, to suffer shame or humiliation, mutilation or death. To a culture accustomed to such public cruelty, the notion of prison as a routine place of punishment would simply not have occurred. But despite the apparently contrary nature of these two approaches to offenders, both are related to underlying principles of great persistence in human affairs.

The maiming of offenders is a brutal way of conveying messages and issuing warnings. Its effect, like that of the wind which changes during a child's grimace, is to fix on the face forever the record of a moment's mischief. The offender cannot forget his misdeed because it is now literally written on his face, and others cannot avoid responding to it. Stigma of this sort however was reserved for relatively minor offenders, who were allowed to live out the remainder of their transfigured lives in the company of others. More serious offenders had to be got rid of. The simplest way of doing this was to expel them from those areas where the rule of law prevailed, into those where it did not. These were the forests and mountains and heaths which constituted 'outlawry'; a physical domain amounting almost to a parallel and independent state.

Killing the offender is an even surer way of removing him from a group, community or nation. Individuals who have seriously overstepped some boundary of society, and particularly one of those which are lettered and signposted by the law, can be forced out for good. In the process of their passing into oblivion, they dramatise the existence of the boundary and, in theory, deter the onlookers.[2] Transportation to colonies was an almost equally dramatic way of putting people outside the law. The hulks and then their penological successors, the criminal prisons, represented the next best thing to physical trans-shipment. The people confined in them had plainly been committed into outlawry. The massive walls and gates around them made it only too plain. It was here that the expulsion theme finally converged with that of stigmatisation, and in a curious way, when the two themes met in the form of the prison, they actually exchanged their most salient characteristics. Death and outlawry, hitherto dependent on permanent invisibility for their effect, now took on an ostentatious visibility. Stigma meanwhile passed from the physical realm of split noses, missing ears and brandmarks in the skin, to the less tangible areas of status and biography via the socially damaging consequences of imprisonment. Both developments can be seen as steps into a higher, or at least a more complex level of abstraction, consistent with the increasing differentiation of the social structure; with shifts in the moral density of society; and the articulation of a status system increasingly dependent on the manipulation of symbolic elements for its effectiveness.

Feudal justice applied a simple, push-pull model of status to its victims; alive or dead; present or absent. The judical system which emerged in step with the development of industrial society reflected a less simple world. As the feudal bonds of land-bound allegiance to a single lord broke down, their place was taken, in practice and in popular mythology, by the idea of competition for status, power and wealth. In this market place conception of man's activities, success is the crowning reward of virtues like hard work, frugality and ingenuity, and the ability to take risks. The law has increasingly mirrored this view by defining criminal offenders as having incurred a 'debt to society' and incarceration as representing its 'repayment'. Spectacular winners, on the other hand, as 'credits to society' are publicised to illustrate the possibilities of advancement to positions of great wealth, social standing and influence.

In all of this, education has become one of the keys to success. Education imparts precisely graduated increments of status to those who experience it. Its opposite, in secular terms, is institutionalised in the arrangements which are made to remove status and to demote individuals to lower positions in the social order.[3] Legal proceedings and mental hospital commitments have served a part of this purpose quite effectively for quite a long time. The denunciatory nature of court proceedings and the total deprivations of status imposed by prisons and hospitals on their inmates can only be fully understood by referenc? to the notion of status degradation.[4]

Apart from its illustrative aspects, demotion is also a real necessity in a social system where all are urged to rise and some actually succeed. In such circumstances ways have to be found of actually filling the logical spaces which are left at the base of the pyramid and which are unlikely to be filled in any other way. Rigid caste systems are one way of doing it in relatively static societies; status demotion does the same job for us.[5]

Outlawing, and stigma, and status demotion are not however the only functions of the prison. Human societies are not just physical systems of interaction; they rely also on expressive structures; belief systems, religious ritual and magic. Belief systems act in some ways as prisons of the mind; they fetter and affect the perceptual process, distorting what has been seen and predicting what is to come. Events are defined and redefined, denied or accepted according to their congruence with existing beliefs. Scholarship and the pursuit of knowledge itself is shaped in this way, insisting that starting points for inquiry be anchored in the accumulated work of the discipline; that perspectives drawn from the past be used to interpret the facts of the future. It takes an ignoramus or a gifted deviant to deny the conventional wisdom and light out on unexplored paths.

A minor instance will illustrate the point. When medieval man looked up into the sky, he did not see the rational objects we now call clouds; aggregations of water vapour subject to fairly well known, if not yet absolutely predictable, physical laws. He saw instead the passing armies of the dead; a skyful of ghostly shadows in transit. The thought did not unduly perturb him, and he was able to dispute, in the medieval sense, where exactly the clouds had got to in their perambulation between heaven, earth and hell.[6] The contemporaries of those cloud gazers, sharing similar beliefs were also laying the ideological and physical foundations of the prison system. And those foundations were fundamentally religious ones.

Religion is concerned, amongst other things, with expressions of group cohesion and a 'view-of-man'; his proper place in the order of things; his relationships to the deity, to the world, to other men and to himself and his own actions. Properly internalised such a 'view-of-man' together with lists of pro-scriptions and penalties; right behaviour and rewards; constitutes a powerful mechanism of social control.. The medieval church had as an additional ingredient of its cosmology, a belief in hell, an actual place illuminated for the popular imagination by terrible tales and horrible pictures. There can be no doubt that such a belief held considerable sway over the minds and actions of men. But beliefs do not remain simply figments of the imaginations, they are often expressed in plastic form or recited as liturgy, ritual and drama. In the middle ages the church provided a setting for all of these, all in one place, and all at the same time. For feudal society, the building itself, the abbey, the cathedral or more humbly the parish church, furnished a physical celebration of the ideas behind it. Prisons are also a part of this tradition of solid, social iconography.

The Reformation and the rise of capitalism destroyed the monolithic partnership of mind and body that had marked medieval thought. Religious pluralism led to a weakened belief in hell and encouraged the emergence of alternative views of man. At the same time, growing out of the problem of the wandering unemployed and the developing need for places of incarceration, there arose the Houses of Correction and ultimately the county gaols. Onto these foundations were subsequently grafted the ideas and the architecture of American penal experiments which began in colonial Massachusetts. The Penitentiary, as its name declares, is a religious institution; an involuntary monastery where evil doers are provided with facilities for reflection, repentance and expiation. They were provided in their purest form, in the early years of the nineteenth century, at the Eastern State Penitentiary in Philadelphia. "The Philadelphia system", according to Kai Erikson, "with its emphasis on penitence and solitude, took its major tone from the Quaker feeling that the resources for conversion lay within every man. . . . "[7] The regime became known as the 'separate system', and despite its forbidding appearance it embodied a basically optimistic view of human nature.

The Puritans, for their part, subscribed to an altogether

sterner view of man, predestined to salvation or perdition, and in either case condemned to a ceaseless effort of discipline, self-control, hard work and denial. It is the Protestant Ethic and its adherents fashioned the Auburn System; where "the men were assembled in long grey ranks, forbidden to speak to one another, kept at heavy labor, and subject to constant harassment from the guards . . ."[8]

This came to be known as the 'silent system' and controversy raged as to the relative merits of 'separation' and 'silence'. A version of the conflict, hard work versus repentance, persists into the present day in the form of the custody/treatment dilemma. Can people be cured? And if so, how? Or are they simply to be confined as quietly and economically as possible?

Beyond these doctrinal differences there is the possibility, hinted at by their religious nature, that prisons also serve larger and more latent functions for society as a whole. One of them may well be the literal establishment on earth of a physical analogue of hell, a representation in stone and iron of a weakened religious belief, and designed to serve the same ends of social control. In fine terms the Philadelphia system might be seen more accurately as limbo, and the Auburn system as hell itself, but both remain stations in the lamentable progress of the sinner.

Systems of religious belief, of magic or witchcraft, of myth and of folk wisdom also contain mechanisms designed to deal with the general problem of human suffering and misfortune and particularly that which appears to be without cause or justification. In non-technical, pre-scientific cultures, the areas of experience which lie outside of satisfactory explanation are necessarily greater than in western industrial ones. What such societies lack in the way of scientific knowledge however, they readily make up for by the ingenuity and richness of the explanations they develop for the misfortunes which both commonly and uncommonly befall men and women.

The need to determine causes for adversity and to allocate responsibility for it to some human or extra-human agency, is one which is shared by our own society. Daily news, as it is presented in the media, lists a catalogue of adversities which ought never to have happened. Aeroplanes ought *not* to come down in places other than airports. Vicars ought *not* to run off with their lady organists. Workers ought *not* to be 'idle'; as strikers are habitually described. The opposites of all these unfortunate happenings could be told as positive moral tales, but it is the presentation of the negatives which lends drama, and authenticity, to their daily recitation. At all events, great efforts are made to determine human responsibility for some of these misfortunes and to cast blame where blame is thought due. A whole range of procedures exist to do this: investigations, tribunals, courts, researches, polls, inquests. Since all of them start from the premise that *someone* is likely to be responsible, if only he or she can be located, it is not surprising that violence is sometimes done to the facts in order to arrive at a finding of guilt. The diffuse and confused nature of responsibility in large scale organisations or in complicated man-machine events, such as an air crash for instance, is sometimes ignored or misinterpreted so as to allow the blame to fall on only one or a few named individuals. Just why the need for explanations of misfortune is so culturally widespread, so urgent and so persistent through time is difficult to explain. Peter Berger's view that all social organisation acts as a 'defence against terror', may be as close to an explanation as anything.[9] The idea of free floating malevolence in society is clearly too terrifying to tolerate.

Anthropologists have studied some of the varied forms taken by this basic need, and particularly those which manifest themselves as witchcraft beliefs and accusations. The literature on witchcraft is too extensive to review in detail here, but Mary Douglas has proposed a broad classification of social structures and their allied cosmologies which seems to have some relevance to this analysis of Rule Forty Three.[10] Societies, she says, may be allocated to positions on two independent dimensions; that of 'group', 'the experience of a bounded social unit'; and that of 'grid', the 'rules which relate one person to others on an ego-centred basis'. The sense of boundary that accompanies belonging to a human group can vary from the most attenuated forms found amongst some hunting and gathering bands, to the most emphatic, such as those which characterise some millennial sects and secret societies. And the rules and principles which regulate relations between individuals and groups within these boundaries, however weakly or strongly defined they may be, can vary from the virtually non-existent to the minutely prescriptive. Cross-plotting the two dimensions produces a logical schema within which four broad types of social structure and their associated cosmologies can be located.

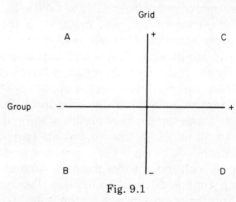

Fig. 9.1

In box 'A' which is characterised by strong grid and weak group, Professor Douglas defines a dual cosmology; a success and ritual dominated sector for the society's elites; and a magical one for the less successful, who may also tend to be attracted to millenarian movements. At 'B' where both group and grid are weak, as in pygmy groups, she suggests the emergence of a 'benign, unstructured cosmos' in which magic, strongly defined symbols and organised religion are either absent or of little importance. Thirdly, at 'C' where group and grid are both strong, she described a 'complex, regulative cosmos' in which ritual is stressed and misfortune is held to be a kind of retribution.

Finally, it is of particular interest to examine what Professor Douglas has to say about social organisation and cosmology at position 'D'. "Within such groups roles are ambiguous and undefined. Leadership is precarious. The group boundary is the main definer of roles; individuals class themselves either as members or strangers. Here the cosmos is divided between good and bad, inside and outside. There is a magical danger associated with emblems of boundary. Group members accuse deviants in their midst of allowing the outside evil to infiltrate. The accusations lead to fission of the group. This is a cosmos dominated by witchcraft and sorcery. It is subject to the vile irrational behaviour of human agents of evil. It is pre-occupied with rituals of cleansing, expulsion and re-drawing of boundaries. . . . It is an irrational cosmos since in it, evil is taken to be a foreign danger introduced by perverted or defective humans.''

The aptness of this formulation to prison society and to the recruitment of Rule Forty Three scapegoats is self-evident. She concludes her analysis of the features to be found in certain African societies, where witchcraft is prevalent, in this way: "In short, if we have social units whose external boundaries are clearly marked, whose internal relations are confused, and who persist on a small scale at a low level of organisation then we should look for the active witchcraft type of cosmology."[11]

The fact that prisons are consciously constructed social forms embedded in a very different kind of society to most of those which are studied by anthropologists, and that the polarities of good and evil are reversed in the case of a prison community, need not deter us from essaying a speculative interpretation of Rule Forty Three in terms of witchcraft and witchcraft accusations. Kai Erikson's thesis in his study of Puritan New England was that offenders fulfil some of the same general functions as witches for society as a whole; i.e. the dramatic illustration of the boundaries around its social spaces and the enhancement of social cohesion amongst majority group members.[12] But the products of these therapeutic purgings no longer disappear into the forests of outlawry; they are systematically organised into social structures which are even more likely than the expelling society itself to generate witchcraft accusations. To take Mary Douglas's definition, there is no social group in our culture with a more clearly marked external boundary than the prison community. The prison wall has been described by Gresham Sykes as, "that line between the pure and the impure", which "has all the emotional overtones of a woman's maidenhood".[13]

The 'magical danger associated with the emblems of boundary' is illustrated by media interest in escapes from prison; in the report of Lord Mountbatten on prison security; by the segregation of Class 'A' escape risks in special units; and even the special blue and yellow patch-work uniform, reminiscent of the fool's motley, which men on the 'E' or escape list must wear.[14] The prison cosmos is indeed firmly divided betweeen good and bad, outside and inside. And whatever the evidence may be from American studies, there is little to suggest that prisons in this country possess clear cut role and value systems to anything like the same degree. The work that has been done here suggests that English inmates are relatively poorly organised into pale versions of American prison subcultures.[15] The existence of Rule Forty Three men in growing numbers can be seen as confirmation of the current pre-occupation of prisoners with 'rituals of cleansing' and the 'expulsion' of 'the evil introduced by perverted or defective human beings'.

There are at least two further questions which must be answered if the witchcraft analogy is to stand up when applied to Rule Forty Three;

1. Why has scapegoating in English prisons apparently increased in recent years?

2. Why are these particular men picked out as scapegoats?

Perhaps the most marked difference between American and English prison life during the last fifty years has been the presence here and the absence there of the silence rule, a lasting memorial to the Auburn system. Its removal in this country is comparatively recent and has been one of the most important influences which have helped to shape the present daily lives of English prison inmates. The abolition of the silence rule has permitted interaction between prisoners on a scale almost as generous as that enjoyed for many decades in the United States. At the same time there has been a growing emphasis on the

rehabilitative pretensions of the system. Basic grade prison staff
have officially disowned the 'screw' or 'turnkey' role in favour
of a more positively therapeutic one.

When the regime was frankly repressive, as it was until the
1950's, any subculture which was able to grow up in the gaps
between the provisions of the official system is likely to have
been strictly oppositional in character. Confrontation with the
official regime stressed and therefore made manifest the boundaries of the inmate society by pressure from both within and
without. Convicts can have been in little doubt about their
identities.

Paradoxically, the alleviation of these pressures, and the rise
of a liberal and humanitarian regime caused confusion and uncertainty amongst the prisoner group. It was no longer clear
who was the enemy. 'Screws', or at least some of them, had
suddenly become 'dutch uncles'. Prison conditions had been
greatly eased in the period after the second world war and there
was even what appeared to be a diminished official concern
about escapes; events which violate the symbolic membrane
that separates 'outlaws' from 'inlaws'. Following publication of
the Mountbatten Report, security was confirmed as a prison
department priority but the overall drift of the system has since
resumed in a gently reformist direction. This gradual abandon-
ment by prison staff of an overtly oppressive stance has pres-
sured the inmate community into action designed to re-assert
its lost identity. And increased opportunities for contact and
co-operation between prisoners have provided the means for
achieving it.

Consensus about positive issues, which can serve to bind social
groups together, is usually achieved only with difficulty, and
often not at all. Given the heterogeneous composition of prison
populations and the evidence about the attitudes which their
members have towards each other and towards those in authority
over them, it would be surprising if they were to agree about
anything in a positive way. Groups of all kinds, whether they
are small, task oriented ones, or large, amorphous ethnic or
national ones, seem to find it easier to achieve cohesion and the

expression of a common identity by agreeing to defile or destroy some hated part of themselves. This seems to be especially the case in the absence of external pressure on the group's frontiers.

The German treatment of the Jews provides an extreme example of the process. Until a few weeks before the Armistice of 1918, it was still possible for the German people to think of themselves as a proud and undefeated martial nation. The sudden collapse of their position, followed by the humiliating terms of ther Versailles Treaty, followed later by the almost total disruption of their economic life, led to the strengthening of deep divisions within the nation. The federation of Germanic States which had been held together in part by common allegiances to a militaristic ethic and by an agressive foreign policy, was suddenly weakened. Politically, the electorate became polarised to extremes and both the left and the right won almost equally massive votes at elections up to the time that the National Socialists finally took power. Once in control of a desperately divided population they set about creating the unity of "ein volk" by a variety of means. Positive symbols were created and propagated as part of a semi-mystical Nordic mythology, and later in the restoration of militarism and expansionist foreign policies. But the divisions were so deep, apparently, and the dispossession of national identity so strong, that only the most massive purging, witchcraft style, of impure internal elements could possibly restore the morale of the German people. Out of that need and the ever-available structures of anti-Semitism, there grew the most hideous and organised hammering of "witches" ever witnessed in history.

As with anti-Semitism so with the treatment of subject black populations by certain white regimes. South Africa's white minority for example is deeply split between Afrikaaners and English speaking settlers. In historical terms they were at war only yesterday. In present political terms about the only common ground between them is their treatment of black people as permanent pariahs who can never be admitted into the 'laager'. Afrikaaner consciousness, significantly enough, symbolises itself as an armed circle of settlers' wagons keeping out the Zulu hordes. A similar analysis could be applied to the racial situation in the United States where prejudice and exclusion have served cohesive functions for a highly heterogeneous and culturally diverse population. Earlier generations had 'found' themselves and affirmed an identity by reference to the frontier of the Wild West; their descendants have had to make do to a large extent with the scapegoating of black people.

Clearly these are not the only elements in the immensely complex position of Jews and Blacks in modern societies but they do appear to define one end of a dimension that extends through all kinds of types of human groupings. Towards the smaller, less organised end of the continuum, the scapegoating of prisoners seems to be a clear example of the achievement of social cohesion by negative means.

Which still leaves the question: "Why are these particular prisoners selected as scapegoats?"

Ceremonies which stress the positive integration of social groupings are often concerned with bodily functions and substances. Christians celebrate their one-ness by symbolically drinking the blood and eating the body of Christ. A significant part of Mary Douglas' work is to do with the use by different cultures of the body and its functions as a language for expressing and comprehending their corporate social existence.[17] She cites the complex rules regulating the behaviour of women in menstruation and the proscription of certain foods, as bodily metaphors for the understanding of particular societies. And just as sex can be used to express positive features of social integration, as in fertility rites, it is also traditionally associated with the treatment of deviants and outcasts. The picture of the Jews castrating the Christian boy, the castration of mob-lynched Negroes, the 'voluntary' removal of testicles from Danish sex offenders, are all details from a long history. Witches too have a sexual side. Old ladies were accused of and confessed to sexual congress with the devil. Most known varieties of witchcraft are also concerned with sexual improprieties as part of a wider concern with the violation of the body's boundaries through its natural orifices, or by tampering with its natural substances.

"The witch himself" according to Dr Douglas "is someone whose inside is corrupt; he works harm on his victims by attacking their pure, innocent insides, sometimes he sucks out their souls and leaves them with empty husks, sometimes he poisons their food, sometimes he throws darts which posion their bodies. And then again sometimes he needs access to their inner bodily juices, faeces, semen, spittle before he can hurt them".[18]

There is an unmistakable parallel between that description and the prison stereotype of the sex offender. As a scapegoat, for a group in search of an identity, he possesses unsurpassable qualifications. He is a present day equivalent of the witch with his 'pipe of ointment' made from the rendered fat of murdered children which enabled him to pass easily through the smallest aperture to do damage to innocent victims. Whose insides could be purer or more innocent than those of pre-pubertal children? Whose evil nature as undeniable as that of their defilers?

So far, if this analysis is correct, it has only explained the beginnings of the rise in scapegoating and the increased use of Rule Forty Three. Even if the volume of scapegoating is taken as an index of social change and confusion, the development of the English prison system has not been so rapid in recent years as to account for a continually rising rate of attack on sex offenders and others. But following the initial surge in recruitment the Prison Department, in keeping with its liberal policy, made special arrangements, first at Manchester and then at Shepton, for Rule Forty Threes to live together, rather than in solitary confinement. The practical effect of this overtly humane policy has been to remove from the segregation cells in each prison of origin, all the men who seemed set fair to spend the rest of their sentences in solitary. Their removal has, it can be argued, left large gaps in the symbolic system so carefully constructed by the inmate group in its effort to come to terms with its own crisis of identity. As a result they have resorted to more scapegoating in order to fill the empty cells. Not wishing to deny these further recruits the benefits of a Shepton-style existence, the Prison Department later adapted wings at Reading and then Gloucester Prison for identical populations of Rule Forty Three men.

It is a simple matter to predict that the filling of the Rule Forty Three status will continue unabated in other prisons until there is more certainty about the purposes of imprisonment and more definition to the relative roles of staff and men. In which case the segregation of Rule Forty Three men to separate prisons may well be a self-defeating policy. Clearly, so far as the Forty Threes themselves are concerned, places like Shepton and Reading and Gloucester are preferable to being left as a helpless 'diaspora' in local prisons around the country. But for the prison authorities it is not clear what they might best do in these circumstances to avoid a continuing escalation of the segregated scapegoat population. Even a policy of separating immediatly on reception all offenders against children would still leave the informers at risk. There is also the possibility that substitute scapegoats would be sought out amongst other types of offenders. The old and the odd, i.e. the 'slags' or even drug offenders, might be chosen to symbolise the impurities which sex offenders now stand for.

It may, in the end, apart from accepting a fixed percentage of men in solitary confinement, be difficult to do anything at all about the expanding numbers of Rule Forty Three cases, without fundamental changes in the nature of imprisonment. And that is unlikely without profound changes in the nature of society itself, for which prison in its present form serves such a useful and continuing function.

Notes

1. See Ralph B. Pugh, *Imprisonment in Medieval England*, Cambridge University Press, 1968. Saxon law did contain references to the primitive uses of prison but following the Conquest it was the custodial function which was uppermost.
2. This discussion draws a great deal on Kai Erikson's elegant chapter 'On the Sociology of Deviance' in his book *Wayward Puritans*, John Wiley & Sons, New York, 1966. See also Michel Foucault, *Madness and Society*, Random House, New York, 1965.

3. The outward appearances of Oxbridge colleges and older prisons are remarkably similar: barred windows, battlements, spikes, massive studded doors with small wicket gates and peep holes.
4. See Garfinkel, *op. cit.*
5. See Louis Dumont, *Homo Hierarchicus*, Weidenfeld & Nicholson, London, 1970.
6. From Marc Bloch, *Feudal Society*, Routledge & Kegan Paul, London, 1962.
7. Kai Erikson, *op. cit.*
8. Kai Erikson, *op. cit.*
9. Peter Berger, *Invitation to Sociology*, Penguin, London, 1972.
10. Mary Douglas, *Natural Symbols*, The Cresset Press, London, 1970.
11. The origins of European witchcraft crazes are located by H. R. Trevor Roper in isolated mountain communities, which share some of these characteristics. See his *The European Witch-Craze of the 16th and 17th Centuries in Religion, the Reformation and Social Change*, Macmillan, London, 1967.
12. Kai Erickson, *op. cit.*
13. Gresham Sykes, *Society of Captives, op. cit.*
14. *Report of the Inquiry into Prison Escapes and Security* by Admiral of the Fleet, the Earl Mountbatten of Burma, HMSO, Cmnd 3175, 1966.
15. As at *Pentonville* described by T. Morris and P. Morris, *op cit.*
16. A policy statement "The Role of the Modern Prison Officer" issued by the Prison Officers Association in 1963 and endorsed by its annual conference, sets out the aim of rehabilitation as a primary concern for basic grade staff.
17. Mary Douglas, *Purity and Danger*, Routledge & Kegan Paul, London, 1966.
18. Mary Douglas, *Natural Symbols, op. cit.*

Bibliography

Ahrenfeldt, Robert H. *Psychiatry in the British Army in the Second World War*. Routledge & Kegan Paul, London, 1958.

Atchley, R. C. and McCabe, M. P. Socialisation in Correctional Communities — a Replication. *American Sociological Review*, 33, 1968.

Berger, Peter. *Invitation to Sociology*. Pengiun, London, 1970.

Bettelheim, Bruno. *The Informed Heart*. Free Press, Glencoe, 1960.

Bloch, Marc. *Feudal Society*. Routledge & Kegan Paul, London, 1962.

Brown, Julia S. A Comparative Study of Deviations from Sexual Mores. *American Sociological Review*, 17, 1952.

Cambridge Department of Criminal Science. *Sexual Offences*. Macmillan, London, 1957.

Clemmer, Donald. *The Prison Community*. Christopher Publishing House, Boston, 1940.

Cline, H. F. and Wheeler, S. The Determinants of Normative Patterns in Correctional Institutions. *Scandinavian Studies in Criminology*. Nils Christie (ed.) Oslo University Press, 1968.

Cloward, Richard A. Social Control in the Prison, in *Theoretical Studies in the Social Organization of the Prison*. Social Science Research Council Pamphlet 15, 1960.

Corsini, Raymond J. Appearance and Criminality. *American Journal of Sociology*, 65, 1949.

Cressey, D. R. ed. *The Prison*. Holt, Rhinehart & Winston, N.Y., 1961.

Cressey, D. and Irwin, J. Thieves, Convicts and the Inmate Culture. *Social Problems*, 10, 1962—3.

Cressey, D. R. and Krassowski, W. Inmate Organization and Anomie in American Prisons and Soviet Labour Camps. *Social Problems*, 5, 1957—8.

Criminal Statistics, England and Wales, 1968. Cmnd. 4098, H.M.S.O.

Douglas, Mary. *Purity and Danger*. Routledge & Kegan Paul, London, 1966.

Douglas, Mary. *Natural Symbols*. The Cresset Press, London, 1970.

Dumont, Louis. *Homo Hierarchicus*. Weidenfeld & Nicholson, London, 1970.

Erikson, Kai. *Wayward Puritans*. John Wiley and Sons, N.Y., 1966.

Farbrother, John E. *Shepton Mallet — Notes on its History, Ancient, Descriptive and Natural*. L.C.P., 1872.

Fitch, J. H. Men Convicted of Sexual Offences Against Children. A Descriptive Follow-up Study. *British Journal of Criminology*, 3, No. 1, July 1962.

Foucault, Michel. *Madness and Society*. Random House, N.Y., 1965.

Galtung, J. The Social Functions of a Prison. *Social Problems*, 6, 1958—9.
Garabedian, P. G. *Western Penitentiary*. Unpublished Ph.D. Dissertation. University of Washington, 1959.
Garabedian, Peter G. Social Roles and Processes of Socialisation in the Prison Community. *Social Problems*, 11, 1963—4.
Garfinkel, H. Conditions of Successful Degradation Ceremonies. *American Journal of Sociology*, 61, 1956.
Giallombardo, Rose. *Society of Women*. Wiley, N.Y., 1966.
Gibbons, Don C. *Society, Crime and Criminal Careers*. Prentice Hall, Englewood Cliffs, N.J., 1968.
Glaser, Daniel. *The Effectiveness of a Prison and Parole System*. Bobbs-Merrill, Indianapolis, 1964.
Goffman, Erving. *Behavior in Public Places*. Free Press, Glencoe, 1963.
Grusky, O. Organizational Goals and the Behaviour of Informal Leaders. *American Journal of Sociology*, 65, 1959.
Hayner, Norman S. and Ash, Ellis. The Prisoner Community as a Social Group. *American Sociological Review*, 4, 1939.
Haynes, F. E. The Sociological Study of the Prison Community. *Journal of Criminal Law and Criminology*, 39, Nov.—Dec. 1948.
Home Office. *Report on the Work of the Prison Department 1965*. Cmnd. 3088, H.M.S.O. 1966.
Howard, John. *The State of the Prisons*. Warrington, 1777.
Humphries, Laud. *Tea-room Trade*. Aldine, Chicago, 1970.
Lorenz, Konrad. *On Aggression*. Methuen, London, 1966.
Martinson, Robert. Solidarity Under Close Confinement. *Psychiatry*, 30, 1967.
Mathiesen, Thomas. *The Defences of the Weak. A Sociological Study of a Norwegian Correctional Institution*. Tavistock, London, 1965.
Mathiesen, T. The Sociology of Prisons. Problems for Further Research. *British Journal of Sociology*, 17, 1966.
McCorkle, L. W. and Korn, R. Resocialisation Within Walls. *The Annals*, May 1954.
Morris, Terence and Pauline. *Pentonville; a Sociological Study of an English Prison*. Routledge & Kegan Paul, London, 1963.
Mountbatten, Earl of Burma. *Report of the Inquiry into Prison Escapes and Security*. Cmnd. 3175, H.M.S.O. 1966.
Nathanson, E. M. *The Dirty Dozen*. Arthur Barker Ltd., London, 1966.
Polansky, Norman A. The Prison as an Autocracy. *Journal of Criminal Law and Criminology*, 33, May—June 1942.
Polsky, Howard W. *Cottage Six*. Russel Sage Foundation, 1962.
Priestley, Philip. The Prison Welfare Officer — A case of Role Strain. *British Journal of Sociology*, 23, 1972.
Pugh, Ralph B. *Imprisonment in Mediaeval England*. Cambridge University Press, 1968.
Riemer, Hans. *Socialisation in the Prison Community*. Proceedings of the American Prison Association, 1937.
Rose, Gordon. Status and Grouping in a Borstal. *British Journal of Delinquency*, 9, 1959.

Schrag, Clarence. Leadership Among Prison Inmates. *American Sociological Review*, 19, 1954.

Schrag, Clarence. A Preliminary Criminal Typology. *Pacific Sociological Review*, 4, Spring 1961.

Schrag, Clarence. Some Foundations for a Theory of Corrections, in D. R. Cressey (ed.), *The Prison*. Holt, Rhinehart & Winston, N.Y., 1961.

Studt, Elliot. *The Re-entry of the Offender into the Community*. Office of Juvenile Delinquency and Youth Development, U.S. Department of Health, Education and Welfare, 1967.

Sykes, Gresham M. *The Society of Captives. A Study of a Maximum Security Prison*. Princeton University Press, 1958.

Sykes, Gresham M. Men, Merchants and Toughs. A Study of Reactions to Imprisonment. *Social Problems*, 4, 1956—7.

Sykes, Gresham M. and Matza, David. Techniques of Neutralisation. A Theory of Delinquency. *American Sociological Review*, 22, 1957.

Tittle, Charles R. Inmate Organization — Sex Differentiation and the Influence of Criminal Subcultures. *American Sociological Review*, 34, 1969.

Roper, Trevor H. R. The European Witch-Craze of the 16th and 17th Centuries. In *Religion, the Reformation and Social Change*. Macmillan, London, 1967.

Trigger, Bruce G. *The Huron, Farmers of the North*. Holt, Rhinehart & Winston, N.Y., 1969.

Weinberg, S. Kirson. Aspects of the Prison's Social Structure. *American Journal of Sociology*, 47, 1942.

Wheeler, Stanton. Socialisation in Correctional Communities. *American Sociological Review*, 26, 1961.

Wilson, J. M. and Snodgrass, J. D. The Prison Code in a Therapeutic Community. *Journal of Criminal Law, Criminology and Police Science*, 60, 1969.

Wood, Stuart. *Shades of the Prison House. A Personal Memoir*. Williams & Norgate Ltd., London, 1932.

Index